THE DANCE IN ANCIENT GREECE

A DANCE CONNECTED WITH THE CULT OF HERACLES
PERFORMED BY YOUNG MEN IN WOMEN'S DRESS.

In the Museo Municipale, Corneto, Italy. From Jane E. Harrison and
D. S. MacColl: *Greek Vase Paintings*, T. Fisher Unwin, London.

THE DANCE
IN ANCIENT GREECE

BY

LILLIAN B. LAWLER

WITH SIXTY-TWO ILLUSTRATIONS

WESLEYAN UNIVERSITY PRESS

Middletown, Connecticut

FIRST PUBLISHED IN GREAT BRITAIN 1964
FIRST AMERICAN EDITION 1965

PRINTED IN GREAT BRITAIN

FOREWORD

IT has been my aim in this book to present for the non-specialist and the general reader some of the results of the study and research in the field of the ancient Greek dance which have occupied many scholars, from antiquity to the present day. No formal bibliographies have been included, but it is hoped that the notes on the several chapters will prove a guide to readers who may be interested in pursuing the subject further.

Much of the material in the book appeared first in 1962, in the form of an issue of *Dance Perspectives*, under the title *Terpsichore: the Story of the Dance in Ancient Greece*. I should like to express my gratitude to Dance Perspectives, Inc., of Brooklyn, New York, and to its editors, Mr. A. J. Pischl and Miss Selma Jeanne Cohen, for permitting and indeed encouraging me to expand that study into its present form. I am indebted also to the editors of *Transactions of the American Philological Association*, the *American Journal of Philology*, the *Classical Journal*, *Classical Outlook*, and *Classical Weekly* for permission to quote briefly in the book from articles which I have published in those journals, and to Professor George E. Mylonas for permission to quote from my article in Volume I of *Studies Presented to David Moore Robinson*.

I owe a debt of gratitude to the staff of the Library of the State University of Iowa, and especially to Miss Ada M. Stoflet, Mr. Frank Paluka, and Mr. Harlan L. Sifford, for assistance in obtaining illustrations; also, to the various museums and publishers who have kindly granted me permission to use their photographs; and to the staff of the publisher of this book, for much kindness and helpfulness.

The transliteration of Greek words into English always presents problems and invites inconsistencies. In the main I have adopted for the Greek words the best-known English equivalents, e.g. *geranos* and *thiasos*, but *thyrsus*, *sileni*, *tympanum*, *sistrum*. Likewise, titles of Greek plays and other works are presented in their most familiar forms.

With these preliminary words I invite the reader to join me in a contemplation of a great orchestic art—or, as the Greeks would say, 'Come, let us dance together!'

LILLIAN B. LAWLER

State University of Iowa
August 1963

CONTENTS

ILLUSTRATIONS

A dance connected with the cult of Heracles performed by young men in women's dress   *frontispiece*

8

I

AN INTRODUCTION TO THE GREEK DANCE

In all the ages since man's tenancy of the earth began human beings seem to have enjoyed and revered the dance; and certainly no people ever appreciated the dance more than did the ancient Greeks. From earliest times their legends and their literature abounded in references to dancing and dancers, and even at the peak of their civilization, in the period of their highest intellectual attainments, the dance held an important place in their religion, their education, and their lives.

To a Greek the word *orcheisthai* had a much broader significance than does the corresponding English verb 'to dance'. It was used to denote rhythmical movements of many sorts—of the feet, of the hands, of the head, of the eyes, as well as of the body as a whole. A Greek could dance without moving his feet. He could, like the native of Samoa and other lands today, dance in a sitting position. There is a record[1] of one Greek, at least, who danced with his legs while standing on his head; and at times writers actually speak of 'standing in a dance'.[2]

Further, the Greek could, and often did, describe as a dance what we would distinguish as a march or procession, a child's rhythmic game, a ball game, an exhibition of juggling, tumbling, or tightrope walking, or even the gesturing of a tragic chorus. He could, indeed, designate as a dance (and not always metaphorically) the rhythmic movements of animals, of fish, of birds, of trees and flowers in the wind, of rivers, of boats on the waters. 'All the earth will dance,' says Euripides (*Bacchae* 114)—and, to a Greek, it really could.

In the mind of the Greek the dance of human beings was not an art complete in itself. He associated it inseparably with music—as do most peoples today. In addition, he customarily associated it with verse. He often 'danced' poetry, interpreting with rhythmic movements of his hands, arms, body, face, and head the verses recited or sung by himself or by another person. The Muses themselves, we are told, did the same thing: the Muse Erato, says an ancient poet, 'dances with the foot, with song, and with the countenance', and the Muse Polyhymnia 'expresses all things with her hand, and speaks with a gesture'.[3] In such activity the Greeks evolved what they called *cheironomia*—a whole system of gestures and symbolic movements the extent and complexity of which are almost beyond our comprehension. It was not a system akin to the finger alphabet used by the deaf today, but was probably more like the ancient *hastas* and *mudras*, or 'hand poses', used in the classical dance and drama of India.[4] Ancient writers say that its effect, even upon foreigners, was immediate and convincing.

Music, poetry, the dance—to the Greek, then, they were all facets of the same thing, the art which he called *mousiké*, the 'art of the Muses'. In its broadest sense it signified to him all of the education of the mind, and, indeed, the very essence of civilization. A late Greek writer says sadly of the people of an invaded city, 'For them there is no significance in life; they have no dancing, no Helicon, no Muse.'[5]

Some modern scholars have suggested that the dance may be the oldest of all the arts of man.[6] The Greeks, being a people of great intellectual curiosity, also speculated upon the antiquity of the art, and upon how it began. Lucian is one of the ancient writers who trace dancing all the way back to the time of the creation of the universe and the appearance of Eros, god of love. These writers, observing the rhythmical movements of the planets in the sky, regard them as constituting a cosmic dance.[7] It is interesting in this connection that Urania, divine patroness of astronomy, was also one of the Muses, patronesses of the dance. Libanius, following Lucian, elaborates on the idea of a dance of the heavenly bodies, but speaks also of the gods as 'fathers of the dance';[8] they inspire men to assume various characterizations in their dances, he says, even as the gods themselves assume shapes and bodies of all sorts in their divine activities. He implies that the Muses, too, who habitually dance 'with soft feet' on Mount Helicon, had a share in the creation of the dance. Another writer (*Anth. Pal.* 9, 504) attributes the 'invention' of the dance to the Muse Polyhymnia; and the Muse Terpsichore, whose particular province is the graceful art, and whose very name means 'joy in the dance', is also associated closely with its early development.

The story most frequently told by the Greeks about the beginning of dancing upon the earth—a story which became a part of Greek mythology—went as follows: In the early days of the world, before the race of man peopled the land, the Titan Rhea, wife of Cronus, taught the art of the dance to the Curetes, sons of Earth, who dwelt in the island of Crete, and to the Corybantes, who lived in Phrygia, in Asia Minor. This act stood Rhea in good stead later. Cronus, so the legend goes, habitually devoured his children at birth. Rhea fled to Crete, and there her youngest son, the god Zeus, was born. Rhea hid Zeus in a cave, and gave Cronus, instead of the child, a stone wrapped in swaddling clothes. Cronus swallowed the stone, and Rhea placed the baby in the care of the Curetes. They, to prevent Cronus from hearing the cries of Zeus, danced over him a wild, noisy, leaping dance, in which they shouted lustily and beat their swords against their shields. Legend says that they later became priests of Zeus, and that they and their descendants continued their dances for centuries, as cult rituals.

Most of the Greeks seem to have believed that the dance was indeed divinely inspired—a direct creation of the gods, by them revealed to chosen mortals, who then taught it to their fellow men. As a result, practically all their greater divinities, and many of the lesser divinities and supernatural beings also, were often portrayed in literature or art as dancing.

In a metaphorical sense, at least, the theory of a divine origin of the dance is reasonably correct, for a large number of the dances of the Greeks can be traced back ultimately to religious rituals. It is highly probable that not only the major deities, but almost every local spirit or divinity as well, was on occasion honoured with a ritual dance of some sort.

Several of the Greeks, however, had different ideas as to the origin of the dance. In the *Laws*,[9] Plato advances the opinion that the dance arose from the natural desire of the young of all creatures to move their bodies in order to express their emotions, especially joy. Here, incidentally, he proposes an impossible etymology, striving to connect the Greek words *chara*, 'joy', and *choros*, 'choral dance'. But, he continues, the sense of harmony and rhythm, which actually makes dances out of instinctive movements, is the specific gift of the gods (especially Apollo and Dionysus) and the Muses. Elsewhere[10] he suggests the possibility that the dance may have grown out of the imitation of words by means of gestures. Other Greek writers attribute the inspiration for particular dances to various heroes or heroines of history or mythology—or even, on a more mundane level, to the stimulating power of wine!

It is customary in certain quarters to look upon the Greeks as a people of great originality, a race that created a remarkable civilization entirely independently. As a matter of fact, the Greeks took over and made a part of their own culture all sorts of elements which they received from other peoples. Thus it is not surprising to find the Greeks themselves ascribing the origin of several of their dances and dance forms to other nations. We have already noted that they traced their art of the dance in general, and their armed dances in particular, to the Curetes of Crete. Most scholars today are convinced that, in the case of certain dance forms, at least, Crete was truly the instructor of Greece. Similarly, the Greeks attributed their Bacchic and other orgiastic dances to Thrace and Phrygia. There is abundant evidence from many sources that the Greek orchestic art, in its developed form in the classical period, was a fusion of many elements.

The mention of sources brings up a question which, in some form or other, is asked of every modern student of the ancient Greek dance, viz. 'How can we today study an art which flourished so many centuries ago—an evanescent, intangible art, which with its creators has long since passed from the earth?' The answer is that we have a great many sources of information about that art; and, by searching with care, and putting together the separate pieces of evidence obtained from the various sources, we can acquire a tremendous amount of information about it, and about the dancers who practised it.

Our sources are in general of seven different types—literary, metrical, musical, archaeological, epigraphical, linguistic, and anthropological. Like most categories, these overlap to some extent; but in the main they are distinguishable.

Literary sources are very numerous. Almost the whole of Greek literature, in fact, is an informal source for the study of the dance. Nymphs, Graces, Muses, gods, goddesses, demigods, mortals, and even animals dance through its pages, and its very figures of speech abound in echoes of the dance. Such informal pictures are of great value to the student. Accordingly, he who would understand the Greek dance would do well to read widely and deeply in Greek literature, of all periods and all genres, prose and poetry, greater and lesser works alike. However, for actual discussions and precise information he will find most useful the works of the philosophers Plato and Aristotle; the dashing, Raleigh-like Xenophon, soldier of fortune and author; the great traveller and geographer Strabo; the biographer and philosopher Plutarch; the lexicographer Pollux; the rhetorician-humorist Lucian; the diffuse antiquarian Athenaeus; and the sophist-rhetorician Libanius.

Metrical sources are those which give us information about the dance through the medium of the rhythms used to accompany it. Metrical sources are of two kinds: treatises on metrics, by ancient grammarians, and the actual lines of verse to which the ancients danced, wherever these have come down to us.

Scholars today have a good knowledge of Greek rhythms, as a result of the work of the ancient grammarians, over a period of several centuries. In particular, there is extant today a *Handbook on Metres*, an abridgement of a treatise by Hephaestion—a comprehensive summary of the most significant aspects of the subject.

Nor is this all. There are preserved to the present day the words of many Greek songs written expressly for the dance. To be sure, this material must be used with the utmost care. Often the fragmentary nature of the extant dance songs raises obvious difficulties. In other cases the whole metrical scheme may be so complicated as to render doubtful any conclusions based upon one interpretation. In 1871 Hermann Buchholtz published a rather charming little volume[11] in which he scrutinized choral metres and indications of movement in the plays of Euripides, to gain some concept of the tragic dance. Somewhat similarly, Christian Kirchhoff in 1898 attempted to restore the entire dance of Greek tragedy from a painstaking analysis of the metres of the *Hippolytus* of Euripides.[12] However, scholars have regretfully agreed that the findings of both these writers are purely conjectural. In lyrics the Greeks did not always adhere rigorously to a set metrical formula, but frequently used substitutions and variations with great freedom; allowance must be made for these in the dance as well as in song. Also, we must not forget that dancers, especially folk dancers, sometimes keep their own rhythm, quite apart from that of the accompanying singers—a phenomenon which can be observed in the folk dances of the modern Greeks. Nevertheless, metrical sources can furnish information on the tempo and mood of a large number of dances, and even, now and then, give a clue to the actual step used in a given situation. Further, through such features as recurring refrains, balanced strophes, sudden metrical shifts, etc., they can afford some idea of the pattern, or choreography, of the dance in question. Metrical sources are primary sources; and, especially where they corroborate information obtained elsewhere, they cannot be ignored.

Musical sources comprise discussions of music by ancient writers, and also remains of the music itself. In addition, a few of the actual musical instruments of antiquity, chiefly lyres and flutes of various sorts, survive in a good state of preservation.

Many ancient authors wrote on music—some of them on the dance as well. Outstanding among Greek works on the subject is the extant treatise *On Music* by Aristeides Quintilianus. This important monograph treats of the whole field of music, and gives some attention to the dance also. The first book, or chapter, as we would call it, deals with harmony and rhythm; the second, with the moral, educational, and therapeutic values of music and the dance; the third, with the mathematical and scientific aspects of music.[13]

We know that Greek music made use of various 'modes' or scales. The notes were written down, but the musical notation was quite unlike our own. There were two systems of writing music, one (the more important) for vocal music, the other for instrumental music. The former consisted for the most part simply of letters and modifications of letters, placed over the syllables of a song. The instrumental signs were constructed on the same general principle, but were derived from a different form of the Greek alphabet. A few specimens of both types are still extant.[14]

Archaeological sources include tangible objects which have survived from antiquity and which furnish representations of dancing and dancers, and of objects used by dancers. They include statues, figurines, reliefs, mosaic floors and stuccoed ceilings, gold and silver jewellery, carvings on gems and ivory, an occasional votive object, and paintings on both walls and pottery.

Archaeological sources are of prime importance to the student, and serve to render the dance strikingly vivid. But, on the other hand, no sources are so capable of serious misinterpretation. In the first place, they usually have come down in a more or less damaged condition. In the second place, the student must never forget for a moment that Greek art is often deliberately unrealistic, and is concerned with ideal beauty, design, balance, rhythm, linear schemes, and stylization, rather than with an exact portrayal of what the artist saw in life. In the third place, the observer must understand and allow for technical limitations, especially in the work of a primitive artist, and for artistic conventions found in each of the arts, throughout the whole span of Greek civilization. These are not easy facts for the amateur to grasp, and a great many amazing errors have been made by writers on the dance who have tried to interpret representations in Greek art without knowing how to do so.[15] The results are sometimes as absurd as would be similar attempts to interpret modern art realistically.

D.A.G.—B

Early in the development of any civilization the artists are confronted with problems which they cannot solve. In particular, they do not understand human anatomy, and they lack the technical skill to portray the body accurately in various poses. To meet this difficulty, the early Greek painter, and the

FIG. 1. YOUNG MEN IN A KOMOS, OR REVEL DANCE.
In the Louvre. From Maurice Emmanuel: *Essai sur l'Orchestique Grecque*, Hachette, Paris.

Minoan Cretan before him, adopted certain conventions. These became standardized, and were used for a long time— even after the artists had acquired considerable skill, and could have abandoned them. As a result, archaic Greek painters, in depicting standing, walking, and dancing figures alike, show the face in side view, but the eye in full face; the shoulders in front view; the arms often in angular positions, even when it is obvious that curved poses are intended; the legs and feet in side view; and, sometimes, both feet flat on the floor (FIGS. 1, 48). Of course, no human body could possibly assume this pose in detail, and neither it nor the angular arms must be interpreted literally. Frequently only context can determine whether the figure is standing, walking, or dancing.[16]

Also, in all periods of Greek painting the figures portrayed are adapted to the space at the painter's disposal, and poses and details are altered freely to suit the design for that space. If the space is small, a large group of dancers may be reduced arbitrarily to two or three, and these may be portrayed not as engaged in the same movements (although they may in real life be dancing in perfect unison), but with as much variety as possible. If the space to be filled is circular or approximately so, the dancers may be reduced to one typical performer. Further, in all forms of Greek art, movement, if violent, may be toned down and softened. In the archaic period, complicated poses which the artist could not depict accurately are simplified. In both relief and painting the technique is shallow and pattern-like; the figures seem flattened out and pasted side by side, so to speak, with little or no depth or background, and usually little or no overlapping of figures (FIG. 2). These conventions, also, must not be taken literally.

The Greek never solved the problem of perspective. Fore-shortening, too, is quite beyond the artist for several centuries, as is the portraying of a head or a body bent to the side, front, or back (FIGS. 3, 29), and also the problem of depicting, in painting or relief, a line of dancers coming towards the specta-tor. Dancers moving in a circle are frequently shown as in FIG. 4, the six women on the left. Rapidity of motion forward is indicated by the convention of a head turned to look to the rear (FIGS. 5, 24, 30). A turn on the dancer's own axis can be indicated only by the turn of the arms, and, after the archaic period, by the swirl of the garments (FIGS. 2, 4, 43).

Garments are usually not depicted realistically, but as decorative elements. Often in scenes of considerable vivacity the folds of garments are unbelievably regular. The Greek vase painter frequently indicates the presence of a human body beneath a garment by drawing the lines of the body upon the

20

FIG. 2. DANCERS REHEARSING.

In Karlsruhe. From Adolf Furtwängler and Karl Reichhold: *Griechische Vasenmalerei*, F. Bruckmann, Munich.

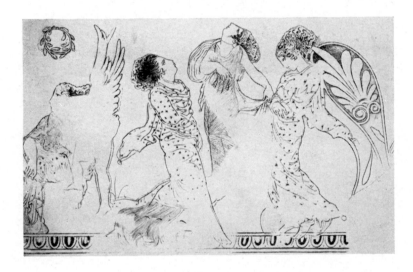

FIG. 3. DANCERS IN A CIRCLE.

In the Louvre. From Fritz Weege: *Der Tanz in der Antike*, Max Niemeyer, Tübingen.

FIG. 4. NOCTURNAL DANCERS IN MOUNTAINOUS TERRAIN.

From Fritz Weege: *Der Tanz in der Antike*, Max Niemeyer, Tübingen.

garment—a convention which often misleads the careless observer to the conclusion that the garment is meant to be transparent (FIGS. 2, 5, 31)[17]—in spite of the fact that in many cases it is obviously a heavy cloak, worn outdoors. Although dancers usually wore shoes or sandals,[18] the artist often suggests these merely by a sole-like line below the foot, or, probably for aesthetic reasons, omits representation of footgear entirely, even in outdoor scenes and in winter scenes, where shoes were certainly worn. In the case of some statues and reliefs, sandals were originally painted on the now apparently bare feet.

The Greek vase painter often draws figures without a 'floor line'—a convention which has led some modern interpreters to insert an imaginary 'floor line' of their own in a given scene, and then to deduce from its position all sorts of untenable conclusions, e.g. that the ancient Greeks engaged in something like ballet, and even toe dancing. Naturally, the observer must use great caution, and avoid all such fantastic interpretations.

It is well for the student of the dance who wishes to use archaeological sources to confine himself to sure representations of the dance in the best period of the dance and of art, when the artists, in full possession of their technique, have relatively little difficulty in expressing what they wish to express. Even then, as he will discover, the artists make use of many artistic conventions. The interpretation of works of earlier periods should be left to experts.

Epigraphical sources comprise the various inscriptions dealing with dancing and dancers that have come down to us. Actually they are archaeological sources, because they are survivors from antiquity, but so distinctive are they that they may be considered a division apart. One of the most interesting of these[19] is a row of letters incised retrograde, or from right to left, around the shoulder of a wine-pitcher dating from about the eighth century B.C., which was found in an Athenian tomb. The pitcher was apparently an award in a dancing contest; it is inscribed 'Whoever of all the dancers dances most spiritedly, let him receive this'. Also of much interest are the great official inscriptions on the island of Delos, where from prehistoric times dancing played a vital part in the solemn rituals at the shrines of Apollo, Artemis, and other divinities. Many of them record the allotment of funds for various objects for the dancers —torches, oil for lamps, branches, garlands, silver and gold platters as awards. Many name unusual dances and performances, e.g. those of marionettes. Other inscriptions, from Athens, Delphi, and elsewhere, record victories in competitions, the equipment and pay of dancers, and the names of distinguished teachers of dancing. Such sources are of great importance. They transmit much curious information, some of it apparently regarded by the Greeks as too obvious for literary recording. They must, however, be interpreted correctly—not always an easy task—and checked where possible with evidence from other sources.

Linguistic sources are the technical words and expressions used by the ancients in speaking of their dances. In many cases the only knowledge we have of an ancient dance form is its name. The names are usually meant to be descriptive; they can, if one strives to comprehend them correctly, give a quick and vivid glimpse of the dancer in action. There are, for instance, dances and figures called by such names as 'the itch', 'knocking at the door', 'the beggar', 'scattering the barley', 'the piglet', 'setting the world on fire', 'the messenger', 'the snort', 'stealing the meat'. In some cases, however, the Greek name of a dance or a figure is not self-explanatory, and the student must work out its etymology, trace the usage of related words in Greek literature, and employ all the resources of the science of linguistics to clarify its meaning in an orchestic context.

Anthropological sources are comparative materials obtained from a study of the dance among various peoples of the world. In modern Greece and the Greek islands, and along the western coast of Asia Minor, one may come upon what seems to be a striking reminiscence of an ancient dance—and, indeed, the performers themselves may claim that their dance goes back to classical times. However, one must be cautious, for many centuries have intervened. There has been race and cultural mixture in these regions, and there are conspicuous Turkish and Albanian elements in many modern Greek folk-dances. Further, there is no continuity of documentation on the dances, attesting survival from antiquity to the present; and what seems an orchestic survival may be a mere accidental similarity. With equal caution the student may observe a few elements which look Greek, in the folk-dances of southern Italy, Sicily, and Spain, lands settled by Greeks in early antiquity. The tarantella, distinctive dance of the Greco-Italian city of Taranto, ancient Tarentum, may actually be of Greek origin, although absolute proof is lacking; it has no real connection with the tarantula except the fact that both words are derived from the name of the town. In ancient times the Greco-Iberian dancing-girls of Gades (now Cadiz) were famous. Many of the dances taken by the Spaniards to Latin America may once have been Greek; and the student of the ancient dance may find unexpected clarification of a vexed point while viewing a fiesta in modern Mexico or Argentina—or even while watching a public parks programme of folk-dancing in a Latin-American section of New York City.

Lands farther afield sometimes furnish material for comparative study. In Ireland, a *feis*, or great festival of music, dancing, and drama, or a *ceilhe*, an informal evening of song, dance, and story-telling, might shed light upon the early Greek contests in *mousiké*. A play in a Chinese theatre in Hong Kong can offer a solution for a problem in the dance of Greek tragedy or in that of the Greco-Roman *pantomimus*. A series of hand and finger movements in a temple dance in Cambodia or in a dance performance in India can suggest how complicated and subtle must have been the Greek *cheironomia*. This is not to say that there is any traceable connection between these dances and those of ancient Greece.[20] Nevertheless, they may sometimes present to the student, dramatically and convincingly, possible concepts of the dance which in the study, the library, the museum, might never occur to him. Also, they may furnish him with the essential element of motion, so lacking in most other sources.

Modern interest in the Greek dance, and attempts to restore and understand it, go back at least as far as the sixteenth century. The great Italian scholar, Julius Caesar Scaliger, in his treatise *On Comedy and Tragedy*, devoted much space to ancient Greek dances and figures. A little later the Dutch scholar Johannes Meursius put together an alphabetical catalogue of more than two hundred dances and figures, to form his *Orchestra, or On the Dances of the Ancients*. Meursius quoted all pertinent Greek sources with which he was familiar, and some Latin sources as well; translated the Greek into Latin; and added comments of his own, in Latin. Also Musonius Philosophus, in his treatise *On the Luxury of the Greeks*, included a section on the dance.[21] From the days of these three scholars to the present there has been a continuing interest, on the part of dancers, classical scholars, and, to some extent, the general public as well.

In our own time, certain new dance forms which owe some of their inspiration to ancient Greece have attracted wide attention. Many of these were in the nature of a reaction from the rigorous discipline of the formal ballet, from the futility and sterility of the dances of ballroom and theatre, and, incidentally, from the restraints of clothing and manners of the dancers' own day. Few of them have represented serious attempts to study and reproduce exactly any specific dances of the Greeks. Isadora Duncan, for example, one of the leaders in this modern movement, often said, 'We are not Greeks, and therefore cannot dance Greek dances.' Her aim was to draw the dance back to nature. Ruth St. Denis and Ted Shawn devoted considerable attention to dances built upon Greek and Cretan painting and sculpture; but they obviously sought to suggest the pictorial effect of the ancient art representations rather than to restore by scientific scholarship the actual choreography or movements of any particular dance. The 'rhythmic gymnastics' of Émile Jaques-Dalcroze showed the influence of Greek art and of such Greek authors as Plato and Lucian, but he, too, carefully avoided giving the impression that he was seeking to reproduce any Greek dance. And certainly the 'modern dance', as we see it today, shows little relationship to that of ancient Greece.[22]

Some contemporary dancers and writers have over-emphasized and been led considerably astray by the statement in a few late Greek writers that the Greek dance in general is to be subdivided into three constituent elements—*phora, schema*, and *deixis*. Plutarch,[23] in the period of the Roman empire, discussed this subject; but it is evident from what he says that even in his day the significance of the words had become obscured. He defines *phorai* as 'movements (*kineseis*) of body or of mind'. He says that *schemata* are 'poses in which movements end'. He thinks that *deixis* means an actual pointing to something by the dancer—as, e.g., the sky, the earth, people standing near the dancer. His discussion is confused and illogical; evidently Plutarch used as his source an earlier work, now lost, which was not clear to Plutarch himself.

A more satisfactory explanation of the terms may be obtained from a scrutiny of the uses of the three words, and of related words, by Greek writers of different periods, in both dancing and non-dancing connotations.[24] We may consider the *schemata* first. They were proverbially as numerous as 'waves in a stormy sea',[25] and by good luck we have the names or descriptions of a great many of them. The word *schema* itself in non-technical connotations denotes form, shape, appearance, figure, manner, the characteristic properties of a thing, a way of doing something. It is used of geometrical figures, of military formations, of figures of speech, of the phases of heavenly bodies. Among the attested *schemata* in the dance are such things as 'little basket', 'snub-hand', 'hand flat down', 'seizing a club', 'the split', 'tongs', 'go past the four',[26] 'sword-thrust', 'owl', 'two-foot', 'elbows out', 'spin-turn',[27] 'lily', 'bunch of grapes'.[28] Even from these few examples it is clear that the word *schemata* does not mean exclusively 'gestures' or 'attitudes' or 'poses in which movements end', or even 'poses' at all. Some *schemata* fit into each of these definitions, and some do not. Besides, many *schemata* encroach upon the meaning given by Plutarch for *phorai*—'movements'. It would seem that the *schemata* were really brief, distinctive patterns which were visible in the course of a dance, some of them lasting but a few seconds, others longer; some recurring frequently, others used once or twice in a dance, for momentary effect.

The word *phora* is related to the Greek verb *phero*, the underlying meaning of which is 'carry'. Greek writers speak of the

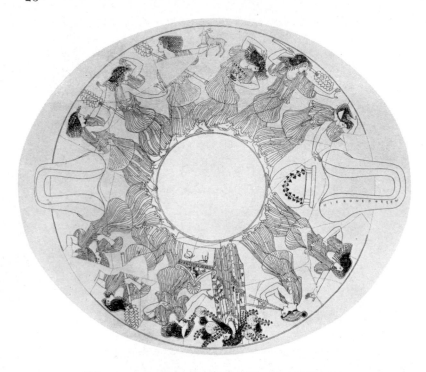

FIG. 5. A DANCE IN HONOUR OF DIONYSUS.
Staatliches Museum, Berlin. From Jane E. Harrison and D. S. MacColl:
Greek Vase Paintings, T. Fisher Unwin, London.

phora of heavenly bodies through the sky, of the wind, of a
missile thrown at a mark, of the waves of the sea. In a dance,
phora would seem to imply 'carriage'. It may be applied to the
feet of the dancer, to his hands, or to his whole body.[29] In
general it would seem to denote the way in which the dancer
carries himself, moves from place to place—a combination, in
fact, of our words 'step' and 'movement'. It would include such
movements as walking, running, leaping, twisting or bending
the body,[30] limping, skipping, hopping, stooping.[31]

The word *deixis* is related to the verb *deiknumi*, 'show, display, portray'. Other related words, *deikela, deikeliktai, deikeli-
stai*, are used to refer to ritual 'mystery' dramas in Egypt,[32] or
to farcical skits in Sparta which portrayed type-characters.[33]

Libanius uses the verb *deiknumi* to mean 'portray' (in the dance) various mythological characters.[34] Quite evidently, then, *deixis* is to be taken not as meaning 'pointing' or 'gestures of the hands' or 'sign language', but rather as denoting 'portrayal' in the dance—of a person, of an animal, of heavenly bodies, of wind, of flame, of flowers. Obviously gesture or *cheironomia* would play a part in such portrayal.

Schema, phora, deixis, cheironomia—these, then, may have served as the framework of the Greek dance, but the life and colour of the dance, its moods and its spirit, transcend any such mechanical analysis. These we can hope to capture only indirectly, and in our imagination; for we shall never, in all probability, be able to restore any ancient dance in its entirety.

II

THE DANCE IN PREHISTORIC CRETE

On the island of Crete, in the southern Mediterranean, there flourished in prehistoric times (about 3000–1400 B.C.)[1] a great civilization, rich in all the arts, and possessed of comforts and conveniences far beyond the dreams of most ancient peoples. By the classical period in Greek history that civilization had already collapsed. It had, however, left some tangible remains in Crete. Also, it had transmitted to the Greeks many cultural influences, and a body of strange tales and legends which became a part of their mythology.

There were stories of a Minotaur, for instance—a creature half man and half bull, who lived in a complicated Labyrinth, and devoured human flesh. There were tales of a great King Minos, who held sway over the Mediterranean Sea and the lands which bordered upon it, and took youths and maidens as prisoners from cities on the mainland of Greece; of a beautiful princess, Ariadne, who fell in love with one of these prisoners, Prince Theseus of Athens, and helped him slay the Minotaur and escape from the Labyrinth; of a mechanical man, Talos, who guarded the island, breathing fire from his brazen nostrils; of Daedalus, the Athenian, who built the Labyrinth for Minos, only to fall into disfavour and be himself imprisoned within its sinister walls.

Paradoxical as it may seem, we of this day and age know a great deal more about this Cretan culture than did the Greeks of the classical period. The explanation of this odd circumstance lies in the amazing work of twentieth-century archaeologists, notably Sir Arthur Evans and his assistants and followers.

The excavation of great palaces and other structures at Knossos and elsewhere has demonstrated that the Minoan

Cretans, as they are usually called, from the name of their most famous king, were not Greeks; their racial connections were rather with Asia Minor. Physically they were a small, dark-haired race, apparently lithe and supple. If we may judge from their art remains, they were a spirited, intelligent people, fond of life and colour and movement, and possessed of a keen sense of beauty. Their costume was distinctive. Men ordinarily wore a modification of a loincloth, and soft shoes or gaiters. Women wore gorgeous dresses of beautifully woven fabrics, cut into flaring skirts and 'bolero' jackets; their breasts were sometimes left uncovered. Women's shoes were dainty, and were occasionally embroidered and high-heeled. Cosmetics were used freely, and hat-like head coverings appear in some periods. Both men and women wore tight belts, apparently reinforced with metal, which produced a characteristic wasp waist. Men and women alike wore jewellery, and affected long hair elaborately curled and arranged.

The chief deity of the Cretans was a great Mother-Earth goddess, a divinity of fertility, apparently identical with the being whom the Greeks called the Titan Rhea. She was worshipped not in temples, but in caves, on mountain-tops, in flowery meadows, on the seashore, in groves of sacred trees, at horned altars, before symbolic pillars, and in small shrine rooms in the palace of the king. Of lesser importance was a god, sometimes thought of as a son of the goddess, sometimes as her consort. Various mythological beings associated by the Greeks with Crete—e.g. Ariadne—are regarded by many scholars as having been actually lesser divinities of the Minoan Cretans.

The Cretans indulged in a variety of amusements. They had instrumental music, singing, and dancing. They seem to have enjoyed watching a hazardous form of acrobatic bull-play, in which both girls and young men took part, and which some scholars regard as a ceremonial dance.[2] On special days they gathered in a 'theatral area' within the grounds of their king's palace, or around a 'dancing floor', to view colourful performances, notably of dancing. To them dancing was of the highest importance, not only as an amusement and spectacle, but as an integral part of their religion.

We have noted the persistent tradition among the Greeks that the Cretans had 'invented' the art of the dance, under divine inspiration; and from the *Iliad* (16, 617) to Athenaeus (14, 630 B) the idea that 'the Cretans are dancers' is a literary commonplace.

Of the actual dances performed by the Cretans, we have specific information on some, and we can make reasonable inferences about others.[3]

The Greeks believed, as we have seen, that the oldest of the Cretan dances, and indeed the oldest dances in the world, were those of the Curetes. These were noisy, frenzied, leaping dances of men, with much attendant shouting and clashing of weapons. Their effect upon spectators was marked. We have noted the legend that they were taught to the Curetes by Rhea, and were first used to drown the cries of her infant son. Thus they were associated from the beginning with religion. The actual identity of the Curetes is something of a puzzle;[4] they may well have been a tribe or subdivision of the Cretan people (one of great antiquity, if we may judge from the story that they were 'sons of Earth') or a hieratic family of 'medicine men' who practised a characteristic dance. As time went on the dances were continued, often by nobles and members of the royal family.[5] Similar dances are attested for Asia Minor, Samothrace, Cyprus, and Rhodes.[6] Probably a variant of the dance of the Curetes in Crete is the dance of the Dactyli of Phrygia, who also were said to have protected the young Zeus, running against one another in a wild dance, clashing shield against shield.

A leaping dance, with much noise-making, is common among many primitive peoples, in all parts of the world. It is not essentially a war dance, but has in general two purposes: (1) to quicken the growing force in nature and induce fertility by restless activity, the high leaps serving as sympathetic magic for the growth of tall food plants; and (2) to frighten away evil spirits with loud and startling sounds. It is thus both a *magic* and an *apotropaic* dance, i.e. in it the performers endeavour by magic to effect something desirable, and to ward off something evil, at the same time.

In its earliest form, the dance of the Curetes consisted undoubtedly of random, uncouth leaps, executed with as much energy as possible, and accompanied by blood-curdling yells. Even in classical times certain Cretan dance-songs were notoriously loud.[7] The dancers and spectators probably clapped their hands or beat sticks together to add to the noise. When the tribe learned the use of metals, the superior noise-making qualities of metallic objects would instantly become evident, and cooking utensils, tools, axes, or weapons would be used as noise-makers. Gradually weapons would be favoured; soon thereafter would come the wearing of armour by the dancers, and the old dance of fertility would have a tendency to become an armed dance. There is no evidence, however, that the dance of the Curetes, as performed in Crete, was ever a combat or war dance.

Occasionally, in Greek writings, we come upon the names of other armed dances of Crete—especially the *orsites*, the *epikredios*, and the *telesias*. The first two of these are mentioned by Athenaeus (14, 629 C) as being in the same category as the Greek pyrrhic dance; apart from this we know nothing of them. They may have been Greek Cretan rather than Minoan Cretan dances.

There is also mention in Greek literature of a Cretan funeral dance, the *prylis*, performed by men in armour.[8] We have little information as to the nature of the *prylis*; however, armed dances or processions around or near a corpse, a funeral pyre, or a burial mound were known to the Homeric Greeks, and it is possible that the Cretan dance was of the same nature. We shall consider these dances in the next chapter.

In addition to the famous armed dances of Crete, we know of many other dances, of varying types. Certainly very old in Crete, as in all lands, were simple circle dances, closed and unclosed. A fragment of Sappho (Frag. 114, Edmonds) says: 'Thus once upon a time the Cretan women danced rhythmically with delicate feet around a beautiful altar, treading upon the soft, smooth flowers of the meadow.' Circle dances, and especially those with hands clasped, have, for all their simplicity, a highly mystical significance among all ancient peoples.

They are often performed around an altar, a tree, a pillar or other sacred object, or around a musician. They frequently enclose a person or an object in a magic circle, to purify it and keep off evil influences. Mackenzie[9] expressed the opinion that at times the Cretan circle dance became a sort of 'skirt dance'. In view of the prevailing costume of the Cretan women, with flaring skirts, it is possible that he was correct, and that on occasion a circle dance of women might be interrupted as the performers released one another's hands and slowly turned, each upon her own axis, while her full skirts swung out in the manner of a 'nautch' dance. Actually some evidence for a dance of this sort has been found. On the wall of the women's living-room in the palace at Knossos there came to light the figure of a charming little lady, with left arm bent at the elbow, the forearm across the breast, and the right arm curving out low from the shoulder. Her long hair swings up from her shoulders on either side, forming the arc of a circle. It seems fairly certain that the figure is a dancer, whirling so rapidly that her hair flies out and up from her shoulders (FIG. 6).

The Cretans evidently believed that their great goddess could be induced by prayer, offerings, and ritual dances to appear to them.[10] Accordingly, the circle dance seems to have become at times an invocation dance, in which women dancers moved in an open circle, with arms upraised. Probable examples are to be seen on Cretan gold rings.[11]

A famous terracotta group from Palaikastro (FIG. 7)[12] shows an open-circle dance of three women, around a male lyre-player. Six clay birds were found with them. The group dates from the period known as Late Minoan III, when Crete had fallen to the Mycenaean Greeks, who had occupied and were ruling the island. Whether the dance portrayed is Cretan or Mycenaean, we do not know. Certainly the figures look Minoan; and birds were sacred to the Cretan goddess. In any case, the group seems to be the earliest extant portrayal in Greek lands of the motif of a lyre-playing male surrounded by dancing women—a motif which among the classical Greeks most often found expression as Apollo and the Graces or the Muses.

FIG. 6. DANCING LADY, FROM A WALL PAINTING IN KNOSSOS.
Sir Arthur Evans: *The Palace of Minos*, Vol. III, Macmillan, London.

There is evidence that in some cases dancers, particularly
women, relaxed a circular formation, formed patterns or designs, and then stood still, so that the goddess and the spectators
might see them. The 'picture' so made would, naturally, have
a symbolic significance. Apparently one of these 'pictures' took
the form of a conventionalized lily or fleur-de-lis (a flower
sacred to the Cretan goddess, and often seen in Cretan art), and
another a bunch of grapes.[13]

D.A.G.—C

FIG. 7. WOMEN DANCING AROUND A MALE LYRE-PLAYER.
Group from Palaikastro, Crete. By courtesy of the Herakleion Museum.

There are a good many representations in Minoan art of men or women with animal heads or masks. One of these, which Evans and Hogarth called the 'Eagle-Lady', portrays a bird-headed, winged woman apparently engaged in a vigorous dance step.[14] It may indicate that the Cretans had bird dances of one sort or another. Other figures, customarily called 'daemons', look like strange men-animals, walking erect in processions.[15] All or some of these figures may represent masked dancers. Also, many scholars believe that a ritual or dance in which the king or priest wore a bull mask may have given rise to the legend of the Minotaur.[16]

Among later Greek writers there is a persistent tradition of a maze or labyrinth dance in Crete, in which the dancers pursued a winding course suggestive of the devious passages of a maze. The fact that the palace at Knossos, called 'the palace of Minos' by Sir Arthur Evans, is complex in plan and suggests the Labyrinth of legend, perhaps lends some support to this tradition. Dances of the maze type are common to many early peoples, in various parts of the world, whether they have labyrinthine buildings or not. Some historians trace them all to a very primitive dance form which is really an imitation of the crawling of a serpent.[17] The importance of the snake in the Minoan religion is well attested, and it is possible that in primitive times a python or other large snake (from Egypt) was kept as an embodiment of the goddess. Some students think that a snake-line dance was performed in the gloom of the many caves in the mountains near Knossos, and that it was climaxed by the exhibition of a living python. Such a performance would have been weird and spectacular in the highest degree.

Certain figurines indicate also that there were in Crete snake-handling rituals, in which women votaries carried small living snakes in their hands (FIG. 8).[18] Earlier, such figurines were interpreted as 'snake goddesses', but recent studies have shown that they portray worshippers, dancers, or priestesses.[19] Snake-handling rituals in the United States and in other parts of the world are usually accompanied with shouts and hymns, and with a shuffling sort of dance.

Similar in appearance to snake-carrying dances are garland-carrying dances—and, indeed, the latter may have been a development from the former. We have definite evidence that in ancient Crete there was celebrated a festival called the Hellotia, in which a huge garland of myrtle was carried in procession. A garland-carrying dance seems also to have been performed in honour of the goddess or spirit of childbirth, Eileithyia.[20]

Another Cretan dance in which objects were carried in procession is the one depicted in relief on the famous Harvester Vase (FIGS. 9, 10, 11). Scholars have differed in their interpretation of the scene, but the most plausible explanation would seem to be that it depicts a harvest festival, with song and dance and general merriment. The men of the village swing along four abreast, in step, their legs raised high, with bent knees, at every stride. Over their shoulders they carry long objects which may be sheaves, tools, weapons, or flails. Three girl choristers sing, and a man shakes a *sistrum* (an Egyptian musical instrument, which is in essence a metal rattle). One of the men dancers stoops down and dances in a crouching position, striking the earth—as dancers do even today in Crete, during

FIG. 8. ATTENDANT OR VOTARY OF THE
CRETAN GODDESS.

Reproduction. Original found in the Palace at Knossos, Crete; in the Museum at Herakleion, Crete.

the village festivals—to stir the earth to renewed production.

Akin to the harvest dance is the dance or procession of the first-fruits, in which a few grains of all the food crops are offered to the goddess of fertility. Some of the actual vessels

37

FIGS. 9, 10, 11. THE SO-CALLED 'HARVESTER VASE', CRETE.
By courtesy of the Herakleion Museum.

used, called by the Greeks *kernoi*, have been found in Crete.
A vessel of the same type is still used today, for the blessing of
the first-fruits, in the Greek Orthodox Church.[21] In Greek
times there was a dance called the 'kernos-carrier'—*kernophoros*
or *kernophoron orchema*.[22] Athenaeus tells us that this dance was
ecstatic, thereby implying a ritual of joy and exuberance
similar to that on the Harvester Vase.

Another gift-carrying procession, to music, shown on a mural
painting at Knossos,[23] was evidently an important processional
dance in honour of the king or the goddess. In it young men of
high station carry large cups and vases.

Rites to a fertility deity often become ecstatic or frenzied,
i.e. the dancer passes into a sort of delirium or trance, and
believes that the deity has taken possession of his body and
mind. In such rites danceis often utter strange sounds and
words which are taken as prophecies and other messages from

the divinity. Dances of this nature, particularly those associated with 'mystery' plays or ceremonies, were well known in Crete; in fact, the Greeks believed that the Cretans had 'invented' such rituals.[24] Some of these rites and dances may have been part of solemn and secret initiations, but we know that many of them were open to all who cared to view them.

We have noted the fact that many rhythmic activities which we should hardly call dances were so considered by the peoples of the ancient world. In this category should be included the ritual swinging of young girls, to insure good (i.e. high) crops. The ritual was part of the classical Greek festivals of the Aiora and the Anthesteria, and is portrayed on Greek vases. In a small domestic shrine in the Minoan city of Phaistos, Evans found a terracotta figurine which could be interpreted only as a girl in a swing.[25] With it were found two side posts, each surmounted by a dove, the symbol of the presence of the chief Cretan goddess; the swinging was thus marked as a religious rite.

Greek authors specifically ascribe to the Cretans the invention and perfection of the 'dance of the tumblers'.[26] From archaeological and literary sources we know that the tumbling dancers were adept at front and back somersaults, flying leaps resembling dives, and rapid kicks. They stood on their heads, stood and walked on their hands or forearms, and bent far backwards in the form of a wheel—all of this, of course, in time to music.[27] Also juggling to music, and, as we have seen, perhaps the acrobatic bull-play, were regarded as dancing.

All such activities presuppose long and rigorous training, and may suggest professionalism in the Cretan dance. In addition, attendants at various shrines, such as the snake-handlers and the armed dancers, must have become very skilful, through long practice, at particular rituals and dances. In Greek days such a band of votaries was sometimes called a *thiasos*. The word is not Greek; it may have been handed down to the Greeks from the Cretans.

There are several other dances and song-dance types which were used extensively by the Greeks, but which were regarded by them as of Cretan origin. Among these are the *hyporchema*, the *nomos*, the *paean*, and the *sikinnis*, which will be discussed in later chapters.

We have noted, in passing, the accompaniment to some of the Cretan dances—the human voice, hands clapped in rhythm, sticks or metal objects beaten together, the Egyptian *sistrum* or metal rattle. To these should be added conch shells and tiny handbells, the hand drum or *tympanum*, metal cymbals, the *syrinx* or Pan-pipe, the single and double flute, the seven-stringed lyre, and the bagpipe.[28]

Such are the facts which we have, or are able to deduce, about the dance in Minoan Crete. It was colourful, rich, spectacular. It undoubtedly influenced the dance of the Mycenaean Greeks, as we shall see in the next chapter, and ultimately, through them, the dance of other Greeks, who came later. Even in classical times the inhabitants of Crete boasted that much of the Greek religion (which would, of course, include the Greek dance) was of Cretan origin. The Greeks called them liars;[29] but the discoveries of modern scholars are proving that to some extent, at least, in this boast they spoke the truth.

III

THE DANCE IN MYCENAEAN AND PRE-CLASSICAL GREECE

OUR attention turns now to the mainland of Greece, where from remote times there had been other settlements and cultures. During the Bronze Age a gifted and energetic race developed there a distinctive civilization, which is usually spoken of as Mycenaean, from the name of Mycenae, its richest and most famous city. It is this civilization that is celebrated in the *Iliad* and the *Odyssey*, in Greek tragedy and other poetry, and in innumerable myths and legends.

In the nineteenth century the Germans Heinrich Schliemann and Wilhelm Dörpfeld did spectacular work in excavating some of the Mycenaean sites; and in our own century A. J. B. Wace, George Mylonas, Carl Blegen, and others have carried this work much further. Within very recent years the epoch-making decipherment of hitherto unintelligible writing of the prehistoric period[1] has proved that the Mycenaeans were actually early Greeks, and that it was they who ultimately conquered and occupied Minoan Crete. In classical times Crete was essentially a Greek island.

Originally hunters and warriors, the Mycenaean Greeks settled at the foot of steep hills, which they fortified into forbidding citadels. Their men were bearded, not smooth-shaven, as were most of the Cretans. Their chief garment was a loose shift or chiton, sometimes covered with a cloak. As their civilization progressed they grew wealthy, and became famous for their work in gold and silver; even the faces of their dead were sometimes covered with death masks of pure gold.

While the sea-power of the Cretans still dominated the Aegean basin, the newcomers on the mainland borrowed a great deal of the Minoan culture. After the Mycenaeans subdued the Cretan cities, the boɪrowing continued. Mycenaean ladies wholeheartedly adopted Cretan fashions in dress, although their male relatives showed greater conservatism in adhering to their chitons and cloaks. Even the religion of the northerners took over some Minoan elements; and sacred trees, caverns, bulls, birds, and serpents were revered much as they were in Crete. Accordingly, it is not surprising to find evidence that the dances of the Cretans, so closely connected with their religion, also influenced those of the Mycenaeans.

The Mycenaeans seem actually to have besieged and conquered Troy, in Asia Minor, as Greek legends insist that they did. The traditional date for the fall of Troy is 1184 B.C.; however, recent studies indicate that 1250 or 1230 may be closer to the real date. After the conquest of Troy, the Mycenaeans seem to have dominated the eastern end of the Mediterranean sea for about a century. Their great cities (except Athens) then fell, probably to the Dorians, less civilized Greeks, who moved down from the north, wielding iron weapons. Some features of the Mycenaean culture, however—including many of their dance forms—persisted, and ultimately fused with the slowly developing civilization which we know as that of classical Greece.

The Mycenaean period is often called the age of mythology. In a sense the term is apt; for most of the legends and tales which form the basis of the artistically developed mythology of the later Greeks are laid in the Mycenaean age, and seem to be racial memories of that eventful period, enhanced by Greek imagination. As it happens, many of the myths mention dancing. Although some of the accounts of dances may be purely fanciful, and others may reflect customs of the authors' own day, nevertheless some may give a picture of real dances practised in Mycenaean times—particularly if there is corroborative detail from other sources.

Myths recount, for example, that the 'heavenly twins', Castor and Polydeuces, invented an armed dance, and frequently performed in it; also that when young men danced in armour in their honour the heroes sometimes appeared and danced with them. Since, as we have seen, there is persistent evidence for an armed dance in prehistoric Crete, we may conclude that there were armed dances in Mycenaean Greece as well.

We have noted references in Greek literature to the *prylis*, an armed funeral dance performed in Crete. Its purposes seem to have been to endeavour mystically to infuse life again into the dead man by a display of physical activity, and at the same time to frighten off evil spirits. The Mycenaean Greeks apparently had a similar dance; later legends claim either Achilles or Pyrrhus, son of Achilles, as its 'inventor'. The latter attribution may have arisen from popular etymologizing, since in classical times the most important of the armed dances was called the pyrrhic dance; the true etymology may rather be from the Greek word *pyr*, 'fire', with an implied comparison of the leaping dancers to leaping flames. A variant of the armed funeral dance seems to have been the encircling procession of chariots and men in armour, like the one in *Iliad* 23, 8–41, or the one around the pyre of Achilles, in *Odyssey* 24, 68–70,[2] and even the chariot race, with a tripod as the prize for the victorious team (*Iliad* 23, 262–623) (cf. FIG. 12). Other rites at funerals were processional dances in which mourners took part, beating their heads and breasts in grief, and chanting dirges and laments.

Dances of maiden choruses, usually in sacred places and in the worship of divine beings, are frequently spoken of in connection with Mycenaean Greece. For instance, the legend persists that when Theseus and his friend Peirithous seized and carried off the youthful Helen, daughter of the King of Sparta (later known as Helen of Troy), she was dancing with other maidens in honour of Artemis Orthia.[3] Similarly, Polymela first attracts the attention of the god Hermes as she sings and dances—'Polymela, beautiful in the dance . . . daughter of Phylas; and the mighty Hermes fell in love with her, seeing her among the maidens singing and dancing to Artemis of the golden arrows . . .'[4] The *Ion* of Euripides, laid in the mythological period, recounts (492–502) the legend of the Agraulides, daughters of a king of Athens, whose shades, after their suicide, used to return and to dance on the grass below the Acropolis,

FIG. 12. GREEK FUNERAL PROCESSION, EIGHTH CENTURY B.C.
By courtesy of the Metropolitan Museum of Art, Rogers Fund, 1914.

presumably in honour of Athena, as they had done while alive:
'where the three daughters of Agraulus tread in the dance the
greensward in front of Athena's shrine, to the shifting strains
of the pipes, when you, O Pan, play upon them in your sunless

cave'. Nymphs, Graces, goddesses, and other supernatural beings likewise dance in choruses, in the myths as they have come down to us. Dances of high-born maidens, in honour of Artemis or a similar goddess, were, as we shall see, a feature of Greek life from earliest times down to the Christian era.

Dancing played an important part in wedding celebrations in mythological times—as it does among most peoples, in all ages. In the *Odyssey* (4, 17–19), Telemachus comes to the palace of Menelaus in Sparta, seeking news of his father, and finds a double wedding celebration in progress, in honour of both the son and the daughter of Menelaus. While neighbours and kinsmen feast, a musician moves about, playing the lyre and singing; 'and two tumblers whirled in their midst, as he set the measure with his song'. This performance savours a little of entertainment in a modern night club!

A wedding dance of a different type is suggested later in the *Odyssey* (23, 131–47). After the slaying of the suitors, Odysseus bids Telemachus assemble all the servants in the palace, in clean clothing, and have them begin a gay dance, with much noise and stamping and merriment. Both men and hand-maidens are to dance and to sing, and the musician is to play his lyre loudly. They obey, and the palace resounds with the noise, so that any passer-by, says the author, would assume that Penelope had at last married one of her suitors, and that the wedding dance was in progress.

In the eighteenth book of the *Iliad*, in the lengthy description of the armour of Achilles, three dances are described as depicted upon the shield. The first of the three (lines 490–6) is another wedding dance: '. . . And they led brides from their homes up through the city by the light of flaming torches, and much singing of the wedding song arose. And young men, dancers, whirled, and among them flutes and lyres resounded. And women standing, each at her own door, marvelled at the sight.' In a short poem called *The Shield of Heracles*, attributed to Hesiod, there is an imitation of this scene; as the bridal procession moves through the streets, we see charming dances of maidens, boisterous dances of youths, and general merriment and dancing through the whole city.

The second of the *Iliad* scenes is a vintage dance (lines 567–72): 'Young maidens and youths, gay of spirit, were carrying the fruit, sweet as honey, in woven baskets. And in their midst a boy played charmingly upon a clear-toned lyre, and sang sweetly in accompaniment, with delicate voice; and dancers followed along with him, leaping, with song and shouts of joy.'

In the case of both these dances the leaps, whirling, and stamping on the earth are well known fertility motifs, the like of which are found among the wedding dances and agricultural rituals of primitive peoples in all ages.

The third of the dance scenes portrayed on the shield of Achilles is a very famous one (lines 590–606). It is laid in 'a dancing-place like the one which in olden days, in broad Knossos, Daedalus had contrived for fair-haired Ariadne. There youths and maidens of costly wooing danced, holding their hands on one another's wrists. The maidens had soft linen garments, and the youths wore well-woven chitons, faintly glistening with oil. The maidens had fair garlands, and the youths had golden daggers hanging from silver belts. And now they ran around with skilful feet, very lightly, as when a potter, sitting by his wheel, which fits in his hands, tries it to see if it runs. And then again they would run in lines to meet one another. And a great throng stood around the colourful dancing-floor, enjoying the sight; and among them an inspired musician was singing and playing on his lyre, and through their midst, leading the measure, two tumblers whirled.'

Much has been said and written about this particular passage, and the lines are of great importance for the history of the Greek dance. In the first place, we note that the author, in composing the scene, has lost the theme of a static design upon a shield, momentarily, and has been so carried away with his mental picture of the occasion that he describes successive figures in a dance. In the second place, it is evident that two types of dance are here portrayed—a choral dance of youths and maidens, and a tumbling dance of two individual performers. The mention here of both Knossos and the tumblers might indicate a dance handed down to the Mycenaeans by the people of Crete.

The dance of the youths and maidens is distinctive. It is a ritual dance performed with great care, by dancers scrupulously dressed in their best garments. It is made up of a crisp, rapid, circular figure, followed by a movement of two lines in opposition to one another. Whether the two sexes alternated in each line, or whether there were separate lines of youths and of maidens, we cannot determine from the text. However, Eustathius, a twelfth-century Greek commentator, says[5] that they did alternate, standing side by side and hand in hand, and that they thus danced *anamix*, i.e. 'mixed up'. Such a combination of the two sexes in a dance was not common in classical times, but may have been so in the prehistoric period. The dance itself could have been of the 'cosmic' type; we know that the ancients had such dances, mimetic of the movements of the heavenly bodies. Thus the rapid circular figure may have represented the movements of the planets through the skies, and the figure of the opposing lines may have represented the apparent approach of the planets to the earth and to one another, and their subsequent separation. Indeed, Euripides, in the *Electra* (467), speaking of this very shield of Achilles, says there were depicted on it 'ethereal dances of stars'! Quite possibly the dance, or one like it, may be the remote ancestor of modern 'country dances' and 'square dances', including our own Virginia Reel, in which circular formations alternate with figures performed by two lines in opposition.

Because of the apparent *anamix* alignment, the dance which we have just considered has been confused by some ancient and modern writers with an entirely different dance assigned by the Greeks to the mythological period—the famous *geranos*. Plutarch[6] tells us that the legendary Athenian prince Theseus killed the Minotaur with the aid of Ariadne, daughter of the Cretan king. Sailing away from Crete with Ariadne and with the Athenian youths and maidens who had been held captive in the Labyrinth, 'he landed at Delos; and, having set up the image of Aphrodite which he had received from Ariadne, he danced with his youthful companions the dance which they say the people of Delos still perform, an imitation of the winding twists and turns in the Labyrinth, contrived in a certain rhythm

which had complicated turns. This type of dance is called
geranos . . . And he danced it around the horned altar.'
Pollux (4, 101) says that the *geranos* was danced by performers
in a line, and that each end of the line had a 'leader'. Eustathius[7] definitely associates the *geranos* with the Homeric dance
of the youths and maidens, and with Cretan dances. He believes
that all these dances were performed *anamix*, and that Theseus
was the first to introduce such a formation into Greece. An

FIG. 13. THE GERANOS DANCE, AS DEPICTED ON THE FRANÇOIS
VASE.

In the Museo Archeologico, Florence. From Adolf Furtwängler and
Karl Reichhold: *Griechische Vasenmalerei*, F. Bruckmann, Munich.

early sixth-century Greek vase of great beauty, the so-called
François Vase (FIG. 13) shows, in its topmost band of figures,
the *geranos* dance with the *anamix* alignment. The dance was
performed on the island of Delos throughout the Greek period;
indeed, a dance of the same name is found to this day in many
of the Greek islands—but it is not of the same type as the ancient
geranos.

In Greek the word *geranos* means 'crane', and scholars have
for centuries tried to explain the dance with reference to the
bird; but actually there is no record in ancient literature of
any 'bird figures' in the dance at all. Apparently the name is
not the same as that for 'crane', but a homonym, going back to
a known root *ger-*, which denotes 'to wind', as of rivers and
serpents. Inscriptions found on Delos attest, by their mention
of torches and lamps for the dancers of the *geranos*, that it was
done at night. Like so many other old maze dances, it probably
originated as an imitation of the winding path of a serpent. The

inscriptions indicate also that the dancers carried *rhymoi*—a word over the exact meaning of which there has been great controversy. It actually seems to mean 'ropes'; and it is highly possible that in the classical period, at least, the dancers may have carried a long rope-like or garland-like object suggestive of a serpent. The ritualistic carrying of a large snake (or a replica of one) in a dance is not without parallel.[8] As we have noted, the Minoan Cretans seem to have had similar dances; and from them the Delian dance may well have stemmed. As performed by Theseus and his companions in the legend, the *geranos* is clearly a winding maze or 'snake dance', used as a dance of victory.

'Ever dear to us,' says King Alcinous in the *Odyssey* (8, 248); 'are the banquet and the lyre and dances'; and elsewhere in the poem (1, 150–2; 21, 428–30) the dance is called 'the delight of the feast'. After-dinner dances apparently went on for hours. Penelope's suitors, in particular, after feasting, 'turned to the dance and to gay song . . . And as they made merry, dark evening came' (1, 421–4; cf. 1, 150–2; 17, 605–6). Sometimes the suitors even prolong their dances by fire- and torch-light after darkness falls (18, 304–6). One wonders a little at the thought of strenuous dancing after a Homeric feast! Yet strenuous it certainly was.

But it is not only the suitors who engage in after-dinner dances in the *Odyssey*. At the court of King Alcinous the dances are very popular, and are carefully arranged by nine chosen supervisors (8, 258–9). The dancers are highly skilled; there seems to be keen competition among them, and pride in their achievement is a national emotion (3, 248–54). Princes dance, along with men of lesser rank; and, as Nausicaa, the princess, says (6, 63–65), they like to have 'newly washed garments' to wear when they go to take part in the dances.

The young men's dances at Alcinous's court are described in detail. The king calls for the best dancers to come forward to entertain Odysseus, and they do so (8, 250–1).The lyre-player steps into the dancing area. As the music begins, the young men start to dance around him—performing simultaneously, but as separate individuals. They 'smite the ground with their feet', and Odysseus is amazed at the 'flashing of their feet'.

A little later (8, 370–84), Alcinous orders 'Halius and Laodamas to dance alone, since no one was a match for them. And so, when they had received in their hands the fine red ball which wise Polybus had made for them, the one, bending far backward, repeatedly threw it up toward the shadowy clouds, and the other, leaping high from the earth, always caught it with ease before he touched the ground again with his feet. And when they had "warmed up" by throwing the ball straight into the air, then they danced closer to the all-nourishing earth, tossing the ball to each other with great rapidity; and the other young men, standing around the dance floor, clapped their hands in time, and a great noise arose.' It is a little amusing to the modern reader to make a mental comparison of Homeric ball-playing with the current American version of the sport; but Odysseus is filled with admiration.[9]

Ladies of the court also engaged in ball-playing dances, out of doors. When Nausicaa and her attendants have done their laundry in the river, and have eaten the picnic lunch which they have brought with them, they lay aside their head-veils, and begin to play ball rhythmically, singing the while (6, 99–109). Nausicaa is the leader in the song and the dance. Later (115–18) a ball, thrown by Nausicaa but missed by an attendant, wakes Odysseus from the heavy sleep into which he had fallen after his shipwreck. Quite appropriately, when he sees the princess, he tells her that her parents must rejoice when they see her 'entering the choral dance, a young twig so fair' (6, 155–7). Incidentally, we are told[10] that, many centuries later, Sophocles, the great dramatist, himself took the role of one of the attendants in his play *Nausicaa*, and danced the ball-dance with consummate skill.

The story of Circe in the tenth book of the *Odyssey* is of special interest. She is called a 'goddess', and *potnia*, 'mistress, lady'— the latter recalling the epithet *potnia theron*, 'mistress of animals', used of many divinities of animal life. She uses drugs to change men into beasts, and she keeps them in order with a magic wand, *rhabdos*, and with sweet song. Her name denotes a magic ring or circle. A black-figured vase in Boston[11] shows her victims as men with animal heads, in a manner similar to the customary depiction of men engaged in animal mummery. Quite possibly the legend of Circe is a poetized memory of animal dances in an ecstatic, drug-induced ritual in honour of an ancient goddess who presided over animal life. The discovery in Mycenaean art of painted figures similar to the so-called daemons of Crete may corroborate the possibility of masked animal dances in Mycenaean Greece.

There are numerous casual or figurative references to dancing in the epic poems and in works which imitate them. For instance, complimentary epithets sometimes applied to countries or cities mean 'with fair dancing-places' or 'with broad dancing-floors'. Delight in 'sleep and love and sweet song and blameless dance' is universal; and grace in the dance is a distinct personal asset for a man, parallel to prowess in war. Battle is called in the *Iliad* (7, 241) 'the war-dance of fierce Ares'. In the *Odyssey* (18, 193-4), Aphrodite, after anointing herself with ambrosial balm, joins in 'the lovely dance of the Graces'. On the other hand, there is in the *Odyssey* (14, 463-6) a warning against the dance inspired by too much wine— 'crazing wine, which stirs even a wise man to song and to silly laughter, and makes him jump up and dance, and brings out a word which would be better unspoken'.

We come now to one of the most spectacular phases of the Mycenaean dance—viz. dance mania. There is reason to believe that on at least one occasion in the Mycenaean period (and very probably more) Greece was visited with a wave of dance mania similar to that which swept over Europe in the late Middle Ages.[12] Greek tradition is definite upon the subject, and several separate stories are told of it, with differing 'sets of characters'. The most frequently recounted of the stories concerns the daughters of Proetus, King of Tiryns.[13] When the three lovely princesses had grown to womanhood, and were being sought by suitors from all parts of Greece, legend says that they suddenly went mad. They rushed out of doors, and in a frenzied dance ranged over the countryside, singing weird songs, and tearing their garments, unable to stop dancing. Many reasons are given for the seizure, all of them centring upon some offence given to a divinity—to a major goddess, or to Dionysus. Some versions of the story add the detail that the princesses were at the same time afflicted with a leprous disease of the scalp which disfigured them horribly. One of the sufferers perished, but the other two were cured by Melampus and Bias, who 'ran them off their feet' until they dropped from exhaustion. Similar stories are told of the daughters of Minyas, Eteocles, and Eleuther; and the dance frenzy visited upon the women of Thebes by the god Dionysus, when the king of Thebes forbade his worship, is part of the same phenomenon. We shall consider the Dionysiac dances in more detail in a later section.

Dance mania may be induced by pestilence, famine, war— any sort of catastrophic upheaval, when the strains and tensions of life prove too much for human endurance. The hysterical, compulsive dance frenzy spreads through a whole community, and often cannot be checked until it has run its grim course, with the resultant death of many of its victims. Certainly the Mycenaean period had its share of 'battle, murder, and sudden death'. The reference in some of the stories to a disfiguring disease may hint at pestilence also as a possible cause for the mania. It is interesting that the word used of this disease is *knyos*, 'an itch'; among the names of ancient dances which have come down to us is one related to this word, viz. *knismos*, 'itch'.

We have already observed that Crete was famous for 'mystery' rituals and dances. Recent studies and excavations (particularly at Eleusis, near Athens) indicate that such performances were of great antiquity on the mainland of Greece as well, and undoubtedly were practised in the Mycenaean period.[14]

We have noted the possibility that Greek writers, in speaking of the dance in the Mycenaean age, are actually describing or referring to the dance in their own times. However, dancing is in general a conservative art, and there may have been considerable continuity from the Mycenaean period down into the classical era.

The three centuries between the fall of the Mycenaean cities and the first blooming of what we know as Greek civilization

FIG. 14. VOTARY IN BULL'S
HEAD MASK, FROM CYPRUS.
By courtesy of the Metro-
politan Museum of Art. The
Cesnola Collection; purchased
by subscription, 1874–76.

are sometimes called the 'Dark Age' of Greece; but modern
writers have pointed out that the age was probably 'dark' only
because we do not have as much evidence about it as we have
about other periods of Greek culture. We do, however, have
archaeological evidence for the dance in that age.

Some of the oldest and most interesting evidence comes from
the island of Cyprus, at the eastern end of the Mediterranean.
During the Mycenaean and Dark Ages, the island had a civilization akin to that of Greece, but with some influences from the
Phoenicians, Egyptians, Persians, and other ancient peoples. In
this period there were certainly many Greeks in Cyprus.

Among the interesting objects found in Cyprus is a terracotta figurine dating from before 1200 B.C. It portrays a masked
dancer pulling a bull mask from his head (FIG. 14). Figures of a
later period, but of similar style, depict another dancer with a
bull mask (FIG. 15); a dancer removing a stag mask, his own
hair and right ear showing beneath it; and a dancer in a

shaggy garment, who has just taken off a horned animal mask of some kind, and holds it in his left hand.[15] The dancers are usually depicted with human feet. Other objects found are replicas of bull masks or of fox masks. All of the figures were discovered in shrines or temples.

There are numerous Cypriote terracotta groups representing circular dances, many of them of a very early period. One type (FIG. 16) shows three figures in pointed caps and long, straight garments. They face to the centre of the circle, and move around a flute-player. It is impossible to determine whether they are men or women. Another type shows three similar figures dancing back to back, around what seems to be the trunk of a sacred tree. In some cases the circle dancers have

FIG. 15. CYPRIOTE VOTARY WEARING BULL MASK.

By courtesy of the Metropolitan Museum of Art, The Cesnola Collection; purchased by subscription, 1874 –76.

their hands joined, in other cases they move independently of one another.

One of the latest of the Cypriote finds which can be associated with the Dark Age in Greece is a fine bronze bowl (FIG. 17), upon which is portrayed a cult scene. To the strains of double flute, lyre, and hand drum, played by three musicians, six women dance before the image of a goddess; they move hand in hand, and the last one of the group holds a flower. The dancers are dressed in a modification of the Minoan costume; evidently the dance is the old maiden dance, or invocation dance in honour of a goddess—here presumably Aphrodite, whose traditional birthplace was Cyprus.

On the mainland of Greece, pre-classical representations of the dance which have come to light are crude and sketchy, but nevertheless informative. Outstanding among them is a little bronze group from Olympia (FIG. 18), which has been dated in the eighth century B.C. It shows seven nude female dancers moving in a closed circle, with their arms on one another's shoulders, in a formation oddly similar to that of some of the dances of the modern Greeks. The fact that the bronze was found at Olympia would imply that it represents a ritual dance, probably in honour of the mother goddess Hera, who had a very ancient shrine in that place.

During the Dark Age the need of the Greeks for artistic expression found its chief outlet in paintings on pottery vessels. Some of these portray, in a stiff, repetitious, 'paper-doll' style, dances of one sort or another. Around the neck of one of them, the famous Analatos vase,[16] of the seventh century, a group of apparently nude male dancers in a long line, their hands clasped, follow a musican playing a lyre; while towards them, with hands similarly clasped, moves a line of women in costumes suggesting the Cretan-Mycenaean style (FIG. 19). In the clasped hands are branches—which may suggest a dance of victory, or a dance to a deity of vegetation. Some writers have seen in this dance the *geranos* of Theseus and his fellow captives; but the dancers here are definitely not in one line, nor do they alternate according to sex.

On a large number of the funerary urns of the period there

FIG. 16. CIRCLE DANCE AROUND A FLUTE-PLAYER, FROM CYPRUS.
By courtesy of the Metropolitan Museum of Art, The Cesnola Collection;
purchased by subscription, 1874–76.

are representations of mourning dances of various types. In
them, long lines of men, women, and sometimes children file
by, their hands held to their heads in the ceremonial gesture of
tearing the hair and beating the brow in grief; or there are files
of marching men, their daggers at their belts; or there are
combat scenes or processions of horses and chariots, suggestive of

FIG. 17. CYPRIOTE DANCE OF WOMEN, IN HONOUR OF A GODDESS.

By courtesy of the Metropolitan Museum of Art, The Cesnola Collection; purchased by subscription, 1874–76.

FIG. 18. CIRCLE DANCE OF WOMEN, BRONZE GROUP FROM OLYMPIA.

From Ernst Curtius: *Olympia*, Aisher & Co., Berlin.

passages in the *Iliad* (FIG. 12). It is possible that funeral processions and dances remained fairly uniform from Mycenaean times down almost to the classical period.

Other vases show bird dances, snake-carrying dances, athletes exercising rhythmically to music. Also, the eighth-century wine-pitcher already mentioned (see above, p. 21), inscribed as a prize for the dancer who danced 'most spiritedly', attests the fact that there were dancing contests at least that early.

Musical instruments of both the Mycenaean and Dark Age include the lyre, the flute, the hand drum, and cymbals— indeed, some actual bronze cymbals have been found, set up in shrines as offerings to divinities. The favourite instrument seems to have been the lyre—a four-stringed type, in contrast to the seven-stringed lyre of the Minoan Cretans. However, Terpander of Lesbos, in the seventh century, is said to have added three strings, thereby, apparently accidentally, re-creating the Cretan form.

In one way or another, then, we can discover a great deal about the dance in pre-classical Greece. There must have been much orchestic activity, in all the Greek lands, and most of the types of dance to be seen later appear to have been present here 'in embryo' at least. The dances of the Dark Age seem to have developed imperceptibly but surely; and suddenly, watching them, we find ourselves in the classical period.

FIG. 19. DANCE OF MEN AND WOMEN, AS SHOWN ON THE ANALATOS VASE.

From Fritz Weege: *Der Tanz in der Antike*, Max Niemeyer, Tübingen.

IV

ANIMAL DANCES

In all the rich array of colourful and distinctive dances developed by the Greeks, probably no group is more important than that of the animal dances. In the first place, they are very old; in the second place, they are very numerous; and in the third place, they underlie more of the dances of the classical period than even the Greeks themselves suspected.

Primitive man is always very conscious of animals, and very observant of their actions. They are of vital importance to him. They can furnish him with food and clothing—or they can wound or kill him. Some of them are terrifying or uncanny to him; others delight and amuse him. Some he associates with his gods in one way or another—either as fitting sacrifices to them, or as their favoured animals, to be kept sacred and safe from harm. Some he actually worships, as gods in their own right, or as temporary incarnations of gods.

By the time we reach the classical period in Greece, religion is largely anthropomorphic, and much of the barbarity of earlier days has vanished. There is no longer a divine bird, but birds, especially owls, are associated with Athena, and she is indeed often designated as *glaukopis*—literally 'owl-faced'. There is no goddess with a cow's head, but Hera is still called *boöpis*—which *could* mean 'cow-faced', although translators usually render it 'ox-eyed'; and at least once[1] she is even said to be *tauropis*—'bull-faced'. The bull is not worshipped, but it is regarded as sacred to various divinities, and Dionysus in particular is sometimes called the 'holy bull'. There is no serpent goddess, but the snake is sacred to Gê, goddess of the earth, and to other goddesses as well. All sorts of beings of mixed form live on in myth and in legend—Tritons, who are fish-tailed men; Sirens, who are woman-headed birds; Giants, some of whom have serpents for legs; and Gorgons, who have writhing serpents instead of hair.

The Greeks, like other ancient peoples, were aware that some animals do actually dance.[2] Apes, elephants, the cat animals, dolphins, bees, bears, and other animals dance in a wild state. Birds dance, in both solo and group formation, in courtship, to attract prey, and sometimes apparently for amusement.[3] Accordingly, it would seem natural to the early Greek to imitate animals in dance.

Among primitive peoples animal dances are very important rituals. They may be performed to honour a totem, the supposed animal ancestor of a clan; to appease a theriomorphic deity, or one to whom a particular animal is sacred; to lay the ghost of a slain animal or, on the other hand, to seek success in the hunt; to induce fertility in a domestic animal; to gain the characteristics of an animal (the strength and bravery of a lion, for example); to avert injury or death (this is particularly the case with snake dances in lands infested with poisonous serpents). Animal masks or the skins of animals often play an important part in such dances, and are believed to possess strong magical properties.

Primitive animal dances are usually performed in a solemn, ritualistic manner. Over a period of centuries, however, the solemnity of the animal dances lessens, their original significance may be forgotten, and the dances tend to degenerate into pure entertainment. The animal masks indeed may come to be a disguise under cover of which dancers may utter coarse jests and derogatory remarks at the expense of others in the community. One notable exception is to be seen in mystic cults; if protected by the secrecy, mystic atmosphere, and rigorous prescription of detail to be found in a mystery ritual, the animal dance can survive unchanged for centuries.

Very old among animal dances are those in which the dancers portray the flight, descent, walk, and other actions of birds. The grace and beauty of a soaring bird, or its droll motions on the ground, seem to have challenged imitation in every part of the world, from the Stone Age down to the present century. The spectacular Eagle Dance of the Indians can still be seen on many reservations in the United States; and it is not long since a 'Turkey Trot' was a feature even of ballroom dancing.

We have noted the possibility that the Minoan Cretans may have had bird dances, presumably to invoke a goddess; if so, some of these may have descended through the Mycenaeans to the later Greeks.[4]

Owl dances are frequently spoken of in Greek literature— humorous dances, in which the strutting of the bird, the

FIG. 20. SKETCH OF THE BIRD DANCERS ON THE
OENOCHOE IN FIG. 21 OPPOSITE.
From the Journal of Hellenic Studies, London.

twitching and twisting of its neck, and its intent, peering gaze were imitated.[5] We are told that bird-catchers used the dance to hypnotize owls which they wished to capture! Also, there is clear evidence for a cock dance in Greece.[6] On the island of Rhodes there was performed annually a famous swallow procession or dance, in which children, apparently disguised as birds and carrying a replica of a swallow, went from house to house, singing, demanding gifts of food, and threatening to steal the food if it should not be given freely.[7] For the theatre, Aristophanes, Crates, and Magnes each wrote a comedy called *Birds*; also, Aristophanes wrote one entitled *Storks*, and Cantharus one entitled *Nightingales*. In all of these plays the members of the

FIG. 21. DANCERS WEARING BIRD MASKS AND COSTUMES.
Oenochoe in the British Museum.

FIG. 22. MAENAD CARRYING THYRSUS AND SNAKE;
WITH SILENE.

chorus were garbed as fantastic, colourful birds, and, as in all
early comedy, the chorus danced (FIGS. 20, 21). The effect
must have been spectacular indeed.

In the Greco-Roman period, in the ceremonies of the
mystery cult of Mithras, the doctrine of the transmigration of
souls was emphasized, we are told,[8] by means of animal dis-
guises and garments adorned with representations of animals.
Certain of the votaries were called 'Ravens', others 'Eagles',

FIG. 23. MAENAD WITH SNAKE AND FAWN.
By courtesy of the Walters Art Gallery, Baltimore.

'Hawks', and 'Griffins'. Our informants say that in the rituals there was much squawking, twittering, and flapping of wings, as the dignified members of the cult went through their mimetic portrayal of the sacred birds.

As old as bird dances, and certainly as important, are snake dances of various sorts. We have already discussed the possibility that the Cretans had a winding maze dance in which the line of dancers represented (or carried a replica of) a huge serpent. The famous *geranos* of Delos, which persisted to a late period, was apparently a dance of the same type, although its original connection with a snake seems to have been forgotten early, and the Greeks themselves explained the dance merely as an imitation of the windings of the Labyrinth in Crete. Even

FIG. 24. A DIONYSIAC DANCE.

In the British Museum. From Paul Hartwig: *Die Griechischen Meisterschalen*, W. Spemann, Stuttgart.

today snake dances survive. Children playing 'Crack the Whip', their elders in a rhumba line, college students celebrating a football victory—often around a bonfire—all are engaged in 'snake dances' which are almost as old as the human race.

More terrifying to behold are snake-handling dances and rituals. We are told repeatedly that snakes were carried in the wild 'mountain dances' in the cult of Dionysus.[9] (cf. FIGS, 22, 23, 24). In the fourth century the great orator Demosthenes speaks of a contemporary of his, Aeschines, who with his mother participated in frenzied dances in honour of the Phrygian divinity Sabazius, rushing through the streets, shrieking, and 'squeezing big-cheeked snakes'.[10] Olympias, the mother of Alexander the Great, is said to have carried live snakes around in an open basket, to be used in the mysteries of Sabazius. As late as the third century after Christ, St. Cyprian is said to have taken part, at the age of ten, in pagan 'snake mysteries' on the Acropolis, in the worship of Athena, to whom the snake was sacred.[11] The rites in such mystery cults are almost always accompanied by dancing.

Occasionally, in a ritualistic dance, not real serpents, but serpents made of dough, are carried. This custom has been observed in India; it was also a feature of the Greek festival of the Thesmophoria.[12]

Another kind of snake dance is hinted at in connection with the famous shrine of Apollo at Delphi. There the story of Apollo's slaying of the great snake, the Python, was commemorated with a festival, during which there was some sort of mimetic enactment of the combat. The flute music that accompanied this performance was elaborately designed to portray all phases of the struggle.[13] Whether the 'boy' who is mentioned as taking part in the ritual portrayed Apollo, and whether the Python was represented by an actor or dancer, we not know; but the wording of our sources does not rule out such a possibility.

FIG. 25. MARBLE DRAPERY FROM THE SHRINE OF DESPOINA AT LYCOSURA.

In the National Museum at Athens. From Guy Dickins: 'Damophon of Messene' in the *Annual of the British School at Athens Vol. 13.*

A lizard dance or figure is mentioned by several writers. They speak of it as the 'lizard-walk' or as 'flirt the tail'.[14] Autocrates (Frag. 1, Kock) says that this lizard motif is Lydian, and that it is commonly seen in maiden dances to Artemis at Ephesus.

The Greeks may have had 'fish dances' of some sort. Archippus wrote a comedy entitled *Ichthyes*, 'Fishes', in which presumably the chorus of fishes, ludicrously garbed, performed appropriate evolutions. In Roman times we have specific evidence[15] for a dance in which the performer, portraying the sea divinity Glaucus, had his feet covered with an artificial fish-tail and danced upon his knees. Throughout Greek literature the metaphor of 'dancing fish' in the sea is a common one.

There is some evidence also for pig dances. Hesychius

D.A.G.—E

FIG. 26. MASKED WOMEN DANCERS, LYCOSURA DRAPERY
(DETAIL).

By courtesy of the National Archaeological Museum, Athens.

records a dance called *kapria* (s.v.), which should mean 'boar dance', but which he defines as an armed dance. It may have portrayed a boar-hunt; on the other hand, some scholars have conjectured that the word *kapria* may be a misspelling of *karpeia*, the name of an entirely different dance (see page 120). We have already noted that the legend of Circe, who turned men into swine, may represent a memory of ritual animal mummery—pig mummery, in this case. Pertinent here is a small bronze figure in the Walters Art Gallery in Baltimore, depicting a man with a pig's head, crawling on all fours. Among the early Athenian comedies was one called *Swine*, by Cephisodorus, in which the members of the chorus probably executed some kind of porcine gyrations.

Of the second century, perhaps, but recording the cult practices of a far earlier epoch, is the carving on the lower edge of a piece of marble drapery found in the shrine of Despoina, at Lycosura[16] (FIGS. 25, 26). Here eleven female figures wearing animal masks and hooflike footgear run along in a rapid processional dance, to the music of lyre and double flute. One of the women, clapping her front 'hoofs' together, wears a pig mask. The marble drapery seems to be a reproduction of actual embroidered or woven drapery offered to the goddess in earlier times. Despoina, 'The Lady', is an old deity, a 'mistress of animals' or divinity of animal life, similar in many respects to the great Cretan goddess. We know that mystery rituals had a place in her cult, and presumably the 'dancing beasts' portrayed on the drapery participated in them. In the shrine were found also a number of terracotta figurines portraying human beings with animals' heads. Of similar type, but of uncertain provenance, is a small terracotta statuette now in the Louvre; it depicts a woman with a sow's head and with cloven hoofs instead of hands, beating a *tympanum* or hand drum.

An animal of importance to both Greeks and Thracians was the bear. There seem to have been Thracian bear masques in honour of the god Zalmoxis. Among the Greeks, we have incontestable evidence that at Brauron, some twenty miles from Athens, there were, even in the fifth century, very old bear dances in honour of Artemis. These dances were performed by maidens between the ages of five and ten years, wearing shaggy yellow costumes suggestive of bears' hides. We are told that Athenian maidens of good family took part in these dances, and were actually called 'bears', as Artemis herself was called both 'The Maiden' and a 'Bear', *arktos*.[17] Recent excavations at Brauron have revealed the 'dormitory' of the little 'bears', and also, in all probability, the area in which their dances took place.[18]

There were bear dances elsewhere in Greek lands, as well. We have seen that on the island of Cyprus at least one early terracotta statuette of a dancer wearing a bear mask has been found. An interesting lead figurine from the sanctuary of Artemis in Sparta shows a female dancer wearing a bear mask, and in Istambul there is a limestone relief showing a bear-masked dancer.[19] One of the 'dancing beasts' on the Lycosura drapery is also usually interpreted as a dancer wearing a bear mask.

There is a considerable body of evidence for lion dances among the Greeks. Whether there ever were wild lions in Greece proper or not, many Greeks had seen lions in Egypt and Asia Minor, and had been deeply impressed by them; and lion-headed dancers are seen in art representations from the Minoan-Mycenaean period down to Roman times. On the Lycosura drapery one of the masked dancers bears a cat-like head that looks like that of a lioness. Some scholars believe that the figure of Heracles in his lion's skin, so common in Greek art and mythology, goes back ultimately to the art type of a lion-masked votary in a prehistoric cult.

A lion dance is specifically mentioned by both Pollux and Athenaeus. The former (4, 103) designates it as a form of 'terrifying dance'. Athenaeus, on the other hand, includes the lion dance in a list of 'funny' dances (14, 629 F). It may seem odd that a dance could be terrifying and funny at the same time. However, when we remember that in lion dances the world over the dancer interpolates loud roars and sudden dashes at the spectators (compare the Lion's reassuring words to his public in Shakespeare's *Midsummer Night's Dream*, Act V, Scene 1), the explanation is clear. In primitive times the terror inspired by lion dances is real, but as a people becomes more sophisticated the dances become a source of amusement rather than of dread.

In the post-classical period the secret rites of the cult of the Persian god Mithras were called Leontika, 'lion ceremonies'. Certain of the participants, designated 'Lions' and 'Lionesses', roared and otherwise imitated lions in the rituals and dances.[20]

The wolf is an animal that has figured in folklore and superstition for a great many centuries. That the early Greeks had wolf rituals or dances, in connection with one deity or another, seems fairly certain. Some scholars see a wolf mask upon one of the dancing women portrayed on the Lycosura drapery. Lycosura is in a remote mountainous region, particularly rich in reminiscences of an old wolf cult. The name Lycosura itself means 'wolf's tail'. At Delphi one of the priests of Apollo was called a 'Wolf', and probably in very early times wore a wolf mask.

Dancers with stag or deer masks are to be seen in Greek art. Some are on vases, some on gems; but the best examples are terracotta figures found in Cyprus—one removing his stag mask, the other, clad in a rough skin garment, holding his stag mask in his hand. Also, there is mention of a procession of revellers in a Greek community in Sicily, wearing 'stags' horns upon their foreheads'.[21]

Dancers who perform in honour of Artemis, Dionysus, and other divinities are often called 'fawns', are said to 'play the fawn', and frequently are portrayed as wearing a fawn skin. In Thrace, the northern country from which the Dionysiac cult is said to have come into Greece, the fawn was of particular importance in mystery rituals; and on a vase in the National Museum in Athens a Thracian woman, a votary of Dionysus, is shown with a fawn tattooed upon her arm. Such tattooing is mentioned in Greek literature.[22]

Hesychius (s.v.) has a record of a dance called 'the fox'— *alopex*. One of the dancing figures on the Lycosura drapery and one of the Cyprus statuettes seem to wear fox masks. Like the fawn, the fox figures in the ritual of Dionysus in Thrace. Women who participated in Dionysiac dances there frequently wore garments of fox-skins, and sometimes were tattooed with a presentation of a fox. We are told that the Thracian word for a fox was *bassara*; and in Greek and Roman literature a female Dionysiac dancer is often called a *bassara*.[23] On an inscription of the second century of the Christian era, now in the Metropolitan Museum in New York, there is a list of members of a Dionysiac *thiasos*, a company of 'dancers' or members of a late mystery cult. Four of them are ranked as 'Chief Foxes'; two are

men (*archibassaroi*), two are women (*archibassarai*).[24] We have
no information as to the nature of the *alopex* dance; but on the
analogy of the Thracian word and its usage, we may conjecture
that *alopex* may be an alternative name for a dance generally
mimetic of the movements of a fox (compare the modern 'fox
trot'), used first in rituals to divinities of animal life or fertility,
and later in animal mummery, perhaps for amusement.

Also of importance are goat dances. The lively, skipping,
sportive actions of the animal itself must naturally have invited
imitation in the dance. Goat dances seem to have been associated primarily with a ritual of birth, death, and rebirth;
accordingly, they are offered to one divinity of vegetation after
another, over the centuries. After the Thraco-Phrygian worship
of Dionysus or Bacchus entered Greece, most of these goat
dances seem to have passed eventually into that cult. We shall
discuss these dances in the following chapter.

There is a record of a dance called *nibatismos*,[25] which Hesychius says was of foreign origin, and which Athenaeus implies
was Phrygian. Meursius thought that the word should be
spelled *nibadismos*. He cited the words *nibades*, meaning 'goats
on the crests of hills or mountains', and *nibadizein*, 'to imitate
goats', and interpreted the dance as a leaping, skipping dance
imitative of goats.[26] Whether Meursius was correct or not we
do not know. If the dance was really Phrygian, it may be
Dionysiac. On the other hand, the Phrygian word may be
incorrectly transmitted, and there may be no connection whatsoever with goats.

Horse mummery seems to go back to an early level of Greek
culture. In an ancient shrine of Demeter, near Phigaleia, the
statue of the goddess had the head and mane of a horse; Cook
believed[27] that here and elsewhere her ritual dance was a
mimetic combat between votaries and masked men 'dressed in
horse skins and furnished with the emblems of death', and that
the purpose of the rite was 'to secure, by mimetic magic,
immunity from danger'. On the Lycosura drapery at least one
of the dancing women wears a horse mask. Certain Laconian
priestesses of Demeter and Persephone were called *poloi*, 'colts',
and spirited women dancers are often called 'colts', meta-

FIG. 27. BULL-MASKED DANCERS.
By courtesy of the British Museum.

phorically. In some Greek cities the horse dance was carried to the ultimate extreme: real horses were trained to dance to the flute, for entertainment at drinking parties.[28]

The donkey seems essentially comic to us; but in ancient religious practice it was taken quite seriously, and associated with vegetation and fertility, and with music. On the Lycosura drapery one of the dancing women wears a donkey mask.

Among the most important of all animals that figure in Greek rituals are the bull and the cow. We recall that the legend of the Minotaur in Crete is thought by some writers to have been suggested by masked bull dances performed by the king; and probably the use of horns on Cretan altars was connected with the idea of a sacred bull. Figurines from Cyprus depict bull-masked votaries. A fine black-figured vase in the British Museum (FIG. 27)[29] shows three spirited dancers wearing bull masks, hooflike coverings on their hands, and bulls' tails. The bull is associated on occasion with various divinities, especially Zeus, Poseidon, and Dionysus. The cow is associated particularly with Hera, but also with Despoina, in whose shrine in Lycosura figurines portraying cow-headed women have been found.

On the Lycosura drapery, the animal most often portrayed among the masked women dancers is the ram; its characteristically curled horns are seen three times in the dance in honour of Despoina. Also, ram-headed figurines were found in the Lycosura shrine.

The panther was one of the animals sacred to Dionysus. Dancers in his *thiasos* sometimes wear panther skins (FIGS. 24, 28, 29), and many scholars have detected panther-like, slinking motifs in representations of the Dionysiac dance.

Whether there were frog dances in the comedy of Callias called *Frogs*, and the one of the same name by Magnes, we do not know. Ordinarily the chorus of a comedy engages in dances, and the chorus is usually represented by the title of the play. However, in the *Frogs* of Aristophanes the 'frogs' form a subsidiary chorus, and some scholars think they did not even come upon the scene—although one might wonder that Aristophanes would let the opportunity for a hilarious frog dance go by.

Not an animal dance itself, but a figure or *schema* to be considered with dances of that type is the *poiphygma*. Hesychius (s.v.) identifies it as a *schema* of the dance; he defines the related verb *poiphyxai* (s.v.) as 'to frighten off', and gives variants of it as 'puff, breathe, blow'. It is used of the hissing of serpents, and the snorting of animals. Meursius, in his discussion of *poiphygma*, reasonably concluded that the figure was one devised to inspire terror in the spectator. Apparently a loud cry was used, together with a sudden lunge at the observers, as in the lion dances. Such lunges and cries are a feature of most primitive animal dances today—in Africa, in the South Seas, among the American Indians. The animal mask lends anonymity to the dancer: when he rushes at the spectators, roaring, they invariably retreat, with startled cries.[30]

We have noticed that in some rituals and dances the animal mummers are all of one type, while in others the *thiasos* is made up of different 'animals'. The comedy called *Wild Beasts*, by Crates, apparently had a chorus composed of animals of varying species, which, we may assume, did some appropriate dancing.

In this connection we recall two passages in Pindar[31]—one in which Apollo 'laughs to see the spirited prancing of monsters, walking upright', the other in which Bromius, or Dionysus, is 'beguiled also by dancing herds of beasts'.

Pollux (4, 103) mentions a dance called the *morphasmos*, which is defined as 'the imitation of all sorts of animals'. It is listed by Athenaeus (14, 629 F), among 'funny' dances. The name is derived from *morphé*, 'form, shape', and implies a changing of form, or a portrayal of many concepts, one after the other. The legend of Proteus, 'old man of the sea', who when grasped assumed innumerable shapes, may have had its origin in a very early dance of this sort; indeed, Lucian (19) says specifically that Proteus 'is nothing but a dancer'.[32] As we have noted, animal dances in general, even when instituted as a ritual tribute to a divinity, tend to degenerate into hilarity. In late Greek times professional entertainers and buffoons apparently used burlesques of the old animal dances to amuse their patrons.

As the Roman empire drew to its close, pagan dancing and dancers fell more and more under the ban of the Christian Church. In particular, professional dancers, finding it increasingly difficult to make a living in the Christianized cities, left the urban centres and scattered over the countryside. Their successors ultimately became the strolling entertainers of the Middle Ages. It seems fairly certain that these fugitives took with them some forms of the ancient animal dances, for animal masks are common among medieval mummers.[33]

As a matter of fact, animal dances and mummeries have never died out. Traces of them are to be found in most parts of the civilized world today—in folk dances, ballroom dances, children's games. In burlesque form, they still have a place in the modern theatre and circus, and, above all, in motion picture and television cartoons.

V

THE DANCE AND THE DRAMA

PROBABLY no aspect of Greek civilization has aroused more discussion and controversy than has the problem of the origin of the Greek drama. Within recent years, in particular, several writers have questioned the accuracy of statements on the subject which have come down to us from the Greeks, especially those in the *Poetics* of Aristotle. Inasmuch as modern scholars do not agree on any one of the newer theories, and inasmuch as our concern is with the dance rather than with the drama as a whole, we shall here follow in general what may be called the 'traditional' account, and refer questioning readers to various studies in the field.[1]

We have already seen in Greek literature a record of dance mania among women during the prehistoric period. One particular type of frenzied, compulsive dance, the one associated with the nature god known as Dionysus or Bacchus, had a great influence upon the Greeks, and persisted, in some form, at least, for several centuries. Clamorous, barbarous rites, performed by ivy-crowned women in honour of this divinity, were said to have originated in Thrace and Phrygia, and to have spread rapidly over the Greek lands. However, the recent discovery of the name 'Dionysus' on a Mycenaean tablet from Pylos has led to speculation that his cult may have first reached Greece through the Minoans and Mycenaeans; and some scholars think that the worship of this deity was *reintroduced* into Greek lands from Thrace after the Mycenaean period.[2]

In connection with the Dionysiac cult we read of *oreibasia*—a frenzied dance over the mountains and through the woods, at night, in the dead of winter, by screaming women who tossed their flowing hair wildly and brandished torches or *thyrsi*

74

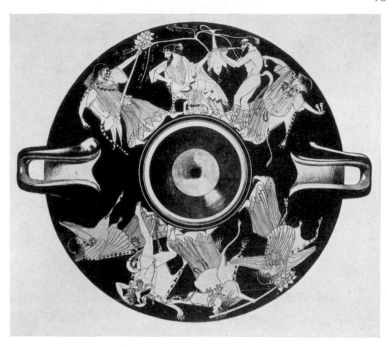

FIG. 28. A DANCE IN HONOUR OF DIONYSUS.

From Adolf Furtwängler and Karl Reichhold: *Griechische Vasenmalerei*,
F. Bruckmann, Munich. In the Pinakothek.

FIG. 29. A DANCE IN HONOUR OF DIONYSUS.

In Cabinet des Medailles, Paris. From Paul Hartwig: *Die Griechischen
Meisterschalen*, W. Spemann, Stuttgart.

(wands tipped with ivy or pine cones). (See FIGS. 4, 22, 24, 28–33.) They are often depicted as heavily cloaked, or wearing fawn skins or panther skins, or having their hands twisted into their garments in such a way as to suggest birds' wings when their hands are lifted. Some of them played on flutes or *tympana*, hand drums. They frequently carried, and occasionally tore to pieces, snakes or small animals of the forest (FIGS. 22, 23). It was believed that the god had actually entered into these women, taking over their minds and bodies, and controlling their actions. Their condition was known as *en-theos-iasmos*, or *enthousiasmos*—'the state of having the god within one'. (Our word *enthusiasm* is a much-weakened descendant!) The women were called Maenads (a name more properly applied to mythological beings, crazed nymphs who were believed to follow in the train of Dionysus) or, more accurately, Thyiades or Bacchantes. Their dance had a marked effect upon by-standers, especially women, who succumbed to the mass hysteria in large numbers.

The violent Bacchic rituals are said to have aroused the intense opposition of many Greek kings, who strove in vain to stop them. Finding themselves powerless against the new cult, Greek leaders seem finally to have succeeded in toning down much of the savagery and terror of the dances, and to have channelled them into formal ceremonies, performed at stated festivals. Certainly in historical times Athens sent a *thiasos*, or group of trained votaries, to present similar dances in alternate years at the festival of Dionysus at Delphi. The dances continued to be performed in this manner down to the second century of the Christian era.

Among the Greeks there were also dances of men in honour of Dionysus as god of fertility and wine. Outstanding among these was the dithyramb—a song-and-dance performance, to the music of the double flute in the Phrygian mode—a feature of the god's spring festival. The participants, in the early days of the dithyramb, at least, had presumably been sampling the gift of the wine-god, for there is a Greek saying, 'When you drink water, it isn't a dithyramb';[3] and Archilochus, in the first part of the seventh century, says that when 'smitten' with wine he

FIG. 30. A DIONYSIAC PROCESSION.

In Naples Museum. From Adolf Furtwängler and Karl Reichhold:
Griechische Vasenmalerei, F. Bruckmann, Munich.

FIG. 31. A DIONYSIAC SCENE.

In the Pinakothek, Munich. From Adolf Furtwängler and Karl Reichhold:
Griechische Vasenmalerei, F. Bruckmann, Munich.

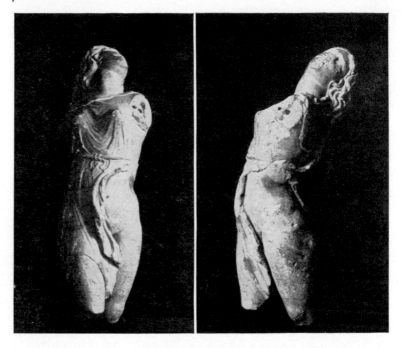

FIGS. 32, 33. DANCING MAENAD, STYLE OF SCOPAS.
By courtesy of Staatliche Kunstsammlungen, Dresden.

knows how to act as *exarchon*, or 'leader', of the dithyrambic dance.[4] Aristotle specifically says[5] that tragedy originated with improvisations of the 'leaders of the dithyrambs'.

In southern Greece, where the early dithyramb seems to have had its best development, the performers were thought of mystically as attendants of the god. Since some of the mythological companions of Dionysus were visualized as satyrs or 'goat-men', and since the goat was one of the animals sacred to the god, many scholars believe that the dancers were called satyrs, and appeared with horned head-dresses, goat-skin trunks, and sometimes footgear contrived to resemble cloven hoofs. Other scholars believe the dancers were always garbed as men, and that the designation of 'satyrs', as applied to them, was purely symbolical. At least one writer[6] thinks that the concept of 'goat-men' as followers of a god may go back ultimately to the partly human, partly animal beings seen in the art of the Minoan and Mycenaean periods.

The ordinary Greek word for 'goat' is *tragos*. In the city of Sicyon, not far from Corinth, there were performed from prehistoric times, in honour of a mythical king, Adrastus, certain *tragikoi choroi*. The name apparently means 'goat dances', but we do not know what they were like, or why they were so called. Some writers think that the dancers wore goat costumes, others that they danced around a sacrificial goat, and still others that the dances were performed in competition, with a goat as the prize for the victor.[7] At any rate, in about 590 B.C. the local ruler, for political reasons, arbitrarily transferred the dances from the cult of Adrastus to that of Dionysus.

The Greeks always called the characteristic dance of their dithyramb the *tyrbasia*.[8] This word is related to *tyrbé*, 'disorder, tumult, revel'. We are told[9] that the early dithyrambic dance was 'full of movement' and 'frenzied'. There must have been a good deal of confusion, horseplay, and improvisation in the performances. Archilochus gives evidence that in his day the songs and dances were fairly riotous, but apparently not frenzied—with some of the participants, at least, happily in their cups.

As time went on, various poets (among them Arion and Epigenes) raised the literary standard of the dithyramb by writing good lyrics for it, eliminating improvisation, and devising and teaching for it a set choreography. It is generally believed that Arion gave to the dithyrambic dance a circular form, with movement around the altar of Dionysus—the form which became its distinguishing characteristic, and from which arose the term 'cyclic chorus', as commonly applied to a group of dithyrambic singers and dancers.

A little later Thespis, of the Athenian deme of Icaria, made epoch-making changes in the dithyramb. He is said to have introduced spoken verse, and to have given the leader of the chorus the role of a character featured in the song and verse. This performer came to be known as an 'answerer', *hypokrites*. Later this word was used to denote 'an actor', 'one who plays a part'. Our word *hypocrite* developed from it.

In the year 534 B.C., Peisistratus, then 'tyrant' or dictator of Athens, established in that city the great spring festival of the City Dionysia. One outstanding feature of the celebration was a contest in *tragoedia*, 'goat song', which was won by Thespis, with his choral group.

By now it was evident that two different genres of poetry were in the making. From the *tragoedia* of Thespis, Greek tragedy is said to have developed. The dithyramb, on the other hand, became a dignified and beautiful choric song and dance.

Beginning in 508 B.C., a contest in the dithyramb, as distinct from the now dramatic *tragoedia*, was a feature of the City Dionysia. Each dithyrambic chorus, consisting of fifty singers and dancers, represented one of the ten tribes of the Athenian people. Five of the tribes sponsored choruses of boys, and five of men. The singers and dancers were trained with rigorous care, either by the poet himself or by a teacher hired for the purpose. The flute player, a highly skilled musician, presumably composed the music. Financial responsibility for the training and costuming of the chorus devolved upon the *choregus*—a well-to-do man who had volunteered or been designated for this service by the officials of his tribe eleven months before the festival. There was much rivalry among the *choregi*, and in the fourth century, at least, there are reports of *choregi* who even used gold in the costumes of their choruses for spectacular effect. Xenophon says (*Oec.* 8, 20) that in his day the cyclic chorus was 'a beautiful wonder to behold'.

On the day of the contest a great crowd assembled in the open-air theatre of Dionysus. At the appointed hour a signal was given by a trumpet, and the performers of the first tribe marched into the *orchestra*, or circular 'dancing-place' of the theatre, wearing their festal costumes and wreaths. They were in single file, in a long line led by the poet or the chorus leader, and followed by their flute-player, playing the specially composed melody. They executed a dignified and graceful circular dance or march around the altar, with accompanying song and gesture, then left the *orchestra* with stately step. After all of the ten choruses had performed, the judges voted. Immediately a herald announced the victorious tribe in the boys' division and that in the men's division. The *choregus* of each winning chorus was awarded a beautiful bronze tripod—something like our 'loving cups' or trophies. After the festival was over, each winning group, with its poet, *choregus*, teacher, musician, and friends, celebrated with a banquet.

The dithyramb continues on in Athens for many centuries, although changing constantly. The number of dancers decreases. There is a growing emphasis on showy solos and elaborate music, until the dithyramb stands almost on the threshold of professionalism. Finally, in the second century of our era, all the tribes unite in a single performance, and the dithyrambic contest comes to an end.

Meanwhile, Greek tragedy had developed far from the simple performances of Thespis, to reach a high artistic level. It was always written in verse. The number of speaking actors became stabilized at three, with each actor taking several parts. The chorus was composed at first of fifty persons; later the number was reduced to twelve, and still later was raised to fifteen. One member acted as leader of the chorus, and was designated the *coryphaeus*—a word which literally means 'head man'.

Like the actors, members of the chorus were always men; frequently they impersonated women. They wore masks. Their costumes were less elaborate than those of the actors, but still more ornate than ordinary clothing. Their shoes were low and soft, to facilitate movement; from the time of Sophocles on, these shoes are said to have been white. The flute player, who walked along with the chorus, wore a long, rich, figured robe.[10] As in the case of the chorus of the dithyramb, the cost of the costumes for the tragic chorus and the expenses involved in the training of the chorus were borne by a *choregus*. In the event of a victory in the tragic competition, the dramatic *choregus* received a crown of ivy; the poet in classical times probably got a money reward.

Throughout the classical period the dance always had an important place in the performance of tragedy; in fact, a tragedy as presented in a Greek theatre was more like an impressive semi-operatic spectacle than a drama, as we use the word today. No less a person than Sophocles, the great writer of tragedy, composed a prose work on the tragic chorus and its dance, presumably in dialogue form. Unfortunately this book has not come down to us. However, we have a great deal of information on the dance of tragedy, from scattered references in the works of various Greek writers, and from comments in the text of the extant plays themselves.

We are told by many writers that the characteristic dance of tragedy was called the *emmeleia*. It was 'noble', and was always carefully adjusted to the mood of the play. Very important in it was *cheironomia*, the code of symbolical gestures. It is said that a trained dancer could portray clearly the whole story of a play by dancing and gesture, without a word.[11]

Originally the chorus entered the *orchestra* at the beginning of the play; later, the entrance of the chorus was often prefaced by a prologue. The chorus came in from the right of the audience, probably singing or chanting, and moving in a solid rectangular alignment of three by four persons when the chorus consisted of twelve, of three by five persons later, when it consisted of fifteen. There could, however, be variations in the entrance to meet the exigencies of the plot. As in the dithyrambic performance, the flute player came in with the chorus.

Arrived in the *orchestra*, the chorus customarily turned and faced the audience, continuing to sing and use gestures until the end of the *parodos* or entrance song. After this, the members of the chorus may have turned their backs upon the audience, to face the actor who now entered. There ensued a dramatic episode, during which the chorus reacted visibly to the speech of the actors, with appropriate grouping, movements, and gestures.

After each episode the actors withdrew, and the chorus, in song and dance or gesture, expressed a response to what they had said, or, sometimes, relieved the emotional tension of the plot with beautiful lyrics. We may recall here that gesture accompanying a song was regarded by the Greeks as a form of dance. Such an interlude is called a choral ode. Like the entrance song, it was accompanied by the double flute. Often the place of one choral ode is taken by a *kommos*—a powerful and moving dirge, sung usually in alternation by the chorus and one or more actors, and accompanied by mourning gestures.

After the final episode comes the *exodos*, or conclusion of the play, consisting usually of the last choral ode, then a brief dialogue, and a few lines of verse sung by the chorus just before, or as, they march out of the *orchestra*. It was customary (with a few notable exceptions) for the chorus to leave as it had entered, in rectangular formation.

There has been much discussion as to whether the word *emmeleia* refers only to the formal, tetragonal, march-like evolutions of the chorus of tragedy, or whether the term covers all the dancing in a play, in the choral odes and elsewhere. We have no specific information on this point, although Suidas (s.v. *emmeleia*) says definitely that the tragic *emmeleia* includes both 'dancing with song and dancing in accompaniment to spoken words'—i.e. gestures.

A scrutiny of the names of *schemata* attributed to the dance of tragedy and of dances indicated in the plays themselves is helpful. We find a *schema* called 'to walk past the four', which might imply the tetragonal type of processional dance; but we also find figures called 'the double', 'flat hand' (probably for slapping), 'hand bent upwards', 'taking hold of the wood', 'the sword thrust', 'the basket', 'fire-tongs', 'tumbling', 'high kick', 'split', 'peering', and others, which suggest definitely a variety of active dances. Also, we know that the Greeks used characteristic *schemata* to express grief—beating the head and breast, and tearing the cheeks, the hair, the beard, the garments. Such gestures are specifically mentioned in the first choral ode in the *Suppliants* of Euripides (71–78), as members of the chorus call upon one another to join in the 'only dance which Hades honours'. We may assume that the same *schemata* would be used in other tragedies, particularly in connection with the *kommos*. We are told that Aeschylus, Phrynichus, and other tragic poets were famous for the invention of rich, colourful *schemata* of all sorts for the dance of tragedy, and that Sophocles himself performed a ball-playing dance in his play entitled *Nausicaa*.[12]

We have in several extant tragedies a definite statement that a dance is now to be performed. Sometimes the leader of the chorus actually calls upon a deity or a Muse or Nymphs to join in or lead the dance—as, for example, in the *Hercules Furens* of Euripides (785–9), where local Nymphs are invited to participate in a joyous *kallinikos*, or victory dance. Other types of dance so introduced into tragedies are various hymnlike processions, simple and graceful dances of women, wedding dances, and, as in the *Bacchae* of Euripides, even the old ecstatic Dionysiac dance itself, with wild running, shouting, tossing of hair, of *thyrsi*, and of torches, and ultimate collapse of the dancers.

One of the most striking of all the dances specificially introduced into tragedy is the mystic 'lyreless' binding dance of the chorus of Furies in the *Eumenides* of Aeschylus (307–96). Nothing like it occurs anywhere else in extant Greek drama. The accompanying song, addressed to 'Mother Night', is written in strophic form, with repeating, incantation-like refrain stanzas. The singers speak of binding the soul of Orestes, their victim, of causing him to waste away, to fall, to be crazed. The weird dance, performed by dancers in the garb of the dread Furies, must have carried with it a breath of savagery. It seems like an echo of actual incantations, which we know existed in some cults. The choreography was undoubtedly circular—although the dancers do not encircle Orestes, who is at the time inside a nearby temple; its gestures were threatening and terrifying.

It is thus evident that free, varied choreographic designs were used frequently in tragedy, and that they must have enhanced greatly the effect of the plays.

Many centuries ago an unknown commentator on a passage in the *Hecuba* of Euripides[13] asserted that on the strophe of a choral ode the members of the chorus 'sang while moving to the right', on the antistrophe (or responsive stanza) 'while moving to the left', and on a third stanza, the epode, 'while standing still'. This statement was for a long time interpreted as referring to the chorus of tragedy, since the comment was made directly upon a passage in a tragedy. Some scholars took the statement as implying a march from left to right across the *orchestra*, then a return in the same way from right to left. Others took it as referring to a circular motion around the altar in the *orchestra*, first to the dancers' right, then to their left. We shall not go into the endless debate on the question. Suffice it to say that the statement is generally discredited today in so far as tragedy is concerned, but that it is regarded as having some validity for the circular dithyramb.[14]

There were undoubtedly many alterations in the dance of tragedy in the late classical period. One change seems to have been the introduction of mute 'supernumeraries' into the chorus. Even before that innovation, the tragic poet Agathon had begun the use of *embolima*—choral songs, with dance, which were not connected with the plot of the play, and could be used as well in one play as in another.[15] In time these interludes were reduced to mere dances, without song. Other changes in the dance of tragedy were necessitated by such developments as the gradual reduction in the size and importance of the tragic chorus, the use of newer musical instruments, and even alterations in the structure of the theatre. By the middle of the second century B.C. all choral dancing seems to have ceased in tragedy, and the choral odes were then sung without dancing. The second-century philosopher Diogenes of Babylon is quoted[16] as saying that since the dance has now disappeared entirely from the drama, there is nothing in the plays that contributes anything to 'the beautiful and the noble'.

As we have seen, a great deal of information has come down to us on the dance of Greek tragedy. However, the exact appearance of those dances eludes us. No director of a Greek tragedy today can claim to set forth an 'authentic' reproduction of the ancient dances. In the case of modern performances it might indeed be well, in order to avoid misconceptions, to inform the audience that the dances are *not* ancient. Also, in devising dances for the plays, the present-day choreographer should in general use dignified, restrained, and beautiful postures and movements, shunning those which are contorted and violent—which the Greeks regarded as 'ignoble' and at variance with the essential character of the dance of tragedy.[17]

In Greece, comedy as a literary form developed later than did tragedy, although many of the primitive performances and rituals from which comedy ultimately evolved were undoubtedly of great antiquity. Among these sources of comedy are usually included vintage revels; phallic or fertility processions; *komoi*, rollicking processions through the streets, especially by young men who were feeling happy after a drinking-bout (FIGS. 1, 51, 52, 53); animal dances and mummery; and impromptu 'village songs' and dances, in which performers (usually masked, to conceal identity) moved from house to house, stopping to revile the various householders in song, with much gusto. Eventually somebody (traditionally Susarion) 'stopped the processions' and staged the performances in a 'dancing-place'. Soon actors, plots, costumes, and masks were added, and comedy developed into a true genre, written in good verse. Thereafter three divisions of Greek comedy are recognized: Old Comedy, from about 480 B.C. to the beginning of the fourth century; Middle Comedy, in approximately the first half of that century; and New Comedy, from that time until the Christian era.

Old Comedy was brilliant and spectacular. Often the plots were fantastically imaginative. The chorus, stabilized at twenty-four members, portrayed human beings, allegorical beings, birds, animals, cities, clouds—all with elaborate costumes and masks. Song and dance were of great importance; in some respects, indeed, a performance of Old Comedy must have borne a resemblance to a modern extravaganza or musical comedy. Outstanding among the writers was Aristophanes; he and his contemporaries revelled in political and personal attacks, and incorporated the popular invective and obscenity of the early processions directly into their plays.

In some respects, Old Comedy resembled tragedy. After a prologue, the chorus entered in a *parodos*; there were dramatic episodes separated by choral odes; the play ended with an *exodos*. Also, comedies, like tragedies, were presented in competition. Unlike tragedy, Old Comedy featured a *parabasis*, or direct address to the audience by the chorus.

The chorus of Old Comedy, like that of tragedy, is said to have been tetragonal. However, it is obvious that in addition to formal marching in a solid rectangle, there was in each play a great deal of spirited dancing of many sorts.

FIG. 34. SUPPOSED KORDAX DANCERS.

In the museum at Corneto, Italy. From Heinz Schnabel: *Kordax*. C. H.
Beck'sche Verlag, Munich.

All our sources tell us that the characteristic dance of Old
Comedy was the *kordax*,[18] performed to the music of the double
flute. Unlike the *emmeleia* of tragedy, the *kordax* is described as
one specific dance. We are told that it was lascivious, ignoble,
obscene, and that its distinguishing feature was a lewd rotation
of the abdomen and buttocks, often with the feet held close
together (FIG. 34). Other *schemata* seem to have been those in
which the dancer kicked his own buttocks, slapped his chest,
thighs, and abdomen, leaped, kicked 'up to heaven', turned his
joints in their sockets, 'spun like a top', and even, on occasion,
beat up his fellow dancers!

However, the *kordax* does not tell the whole story of the
dancing in Old Comedy. The performances were enriched with
colourful dances and *schemata* of many sorts, appropriate to the
plots of the several plays. There were animal dances (many of
the plays bear animal titles and have choruses costumed as

fanciful animals (cf. FIGS. 20, 27), burlesques of religious rituals, dances of sheer joy, victory dances, processions, circle dances, seductive dances. There were dances which purported to represent or suggest those of solemn mystery cults.[19] There is in the *Lysistrata* of Aristophanes (1273-7) an *anamix* dance of men and women—something which must have been not too common a sight in Athens of the classical period. There is even mention of a play, seemingly a comedy, in which the twenty-four members of the chorus appear to have impersonated the letters of the Ionic alphabet, and to have performed some kind of 'alphabet dance'.[20]

Middle Comedy is really but a transition to New Comedy. None of the plays of this genre have survived. They are said to have been similar to Old Comedy in form, but to have been allegorical and even rhetorical, and to have lacked the zest of Old Comedy.

New Comedy is a comedy of manners, with emphasis on plot, and with characters representing 'types' drawn from everyday life. There is in it no chorus such as that of Old Comedy; but between dramatic episodes a group of singers and dancers may enter and perform songs and dances which have no close connection with the plot. Occasionally a solo dance by one of the actors is interpolated, e.g. by a character representing a professional dancing-girl. Within very recent years a virtually complete play of this genre, the *Dyskolos* or 'Bad-Tempered Man' of Menander, has almost miraculously come to light[21]—the only one which has survived intact. There are in it four points at which a song and dance by the chorus is indicated, but no lyrics are given for the songs. At the end of the play the 'bad-tempered man' is dragged against his will into revels, presumably with dancing, which may or may not be shown onstage.

The *kordax* of Old Comedy, however, continued to be performed as a detached solo dance, both in and out of the theatre, down to the period of the Roman Empire. Its lewdness ultimately aroused the ire of the Christians, and the dance disappeared.

The Greeks had various minor comic performances, e.g. Doric

FIG. 35. BURLESQUE OF A 'BASKET DANCE' BY A PHLYAX DANCER.
By courtesy of the British Museum.

farces, mimes, marionette shows, and the '*phlyakes* plays'. The latter, which developed in the Greek cities of southern Italy and Sicily, were hilarious parodies of themes from mythology, tragedy, or daily life, performed by *phlyakes*, masked actors attired in ridiculously padded costumes. There was some dancing in these plays. Vase paintings furnish us such examples as a 'dance with pilfered food', and a burlesque of a ritual 'basket dance' by an actor wearing artificial breasts (FIG. 35).

Late in the sixth century before Christ there had been introduced at Athens a new kind of performance—the satyr play.[22] It had no connection with comedy, but was a distinctive genre. The satyr play was short, was written in verse, and was in general a burlesque presentation of a mythological theme. It was loud, noisy, even riotous, and it made free use of obscenities. Its structure was similar to that of tragedy; and indeed it soon became the custom for each playwright to present one satyr

FIG. 36. THE PRONOMOS VASE, NAPLES MUSEUM. MANY SCHOLARS
SEE HERE A PREPARATION FOR A SATYR PLAY, WITH ACTORS,
CHORUS, FLUTE-PLAYER AND LYRE-PLAYER.
From Adolf Furtwängler and Karl Reichhold: *Griechische Vasenmalerei,*
F. Bruckmann, Munich.

play along with a trilogy of tragedies in the dramatic competition at the City Dionysia. The chorus of twelve men represented
sileni, creatures with the bodies of men, but with horses' ears,
tails, and hoofs. Later there was some modification in the
costumes of the chorus, and some fusion with the idea of goat-
men, or satyrs, attending upon Dionysus. The leader of the
chorus always portrayed Silenus, who was elderly, fat, tipsy,
and snub-nosed (FIG. 36).

As we should expect, the dance had a prominent place in
the satyr play, for the playwright Pratinas, its 'inventor', was
famous also as a dancing teacher. The characteristic dance of
the satyr play, the *sikinnis,* was, like the *kordax* of comedy, a
particular dance, performed once or more within the play. It
was lively, vigorous, and lewd, with horseplay and acrobatics,
and, at times, an affected, mincing gait, together with exag-
gerated movements of the hips and shaking of the whole body.
We read also of 'swift leaps and kicks', stamping, and whirling
turns, the whole accompanied by loud shouts. It made use of
expressive gestures, many of them obscene. Music was furnished

by the double flute, and also, to a lesser extent, the lyre.

As in comedy, dances other than the characteristic one apparently were used also in the satyr plays—victory dances, for example, an occasional wedding dance, and perhaps burlesques of tragic dances.

After the third century B.C. the satyr play seems to have been more popular outside Athens than in that city. In many parts of the Greco-Roman world satyr plays were produced down to the beginning of the Christian era. The plays must have changed considerably, to suit changing tastes, but it is possible that the nature of the *sikinnis* remained approximately the same throughout its history. Its pagan obscenities were eventually suppressed by the Christians.

VI

OTHER ORGIASTIC AND MYSTERY
DANCES

THROUGHOUT their history the Greeks displayed deep interest in esoteric religious rites, practically all of which included dancing. Frequently these rites involved also initiation into so-called 'mysteries', some of which were concerned with fertility, and in many of which there was imparted to the worshipper secret information on how he might secure for himself a happy life after death.

We have already considered the orgiastic rituals associated with the worship of Dionysus or Bacchus, and also those which involved animal dances. But there were many more, especially in the cults of fertility deities.

Artemis was a goddess who presided over various aspects of life, among them fertility. At the shrine of Artemis Limnatis, in southern Greece, choruses of young girls sang and danced in honour of the goddess. Votive *tympana* found at this shrine are evidence that some of the dances, at least, were orgiastic; for the insistent beating of the *tympanum* was characteristic of such dances, and was indeed instrumental in inducing the frenzied state of mind deemed necessary for them. In Sparta, we are told, girls and young women came to the shrine of Artemis and performed unrestrained, ecstatic dances to the goddess 'wearing only one chiton'[1]—that is, clad in the short tunic which usually was worn beneath the long outer dress. In connection with the great temple of Artemis at Ephesus, in Asia Minor, there is mention of mysteries in which maiden priestesses participated, engaging in ecstatic dances.[2] At Ancyra, also in Asia Minor, we hear of women performing dances which are likened to 'Bacchic orgies'—not only in the cult of Artemis, but in that of Athena

92

as well.[3] In other ecstatic rites to Artemis, chiefly in southern Greece, Apollo as fertility god is invoked along with his sister goddess.

Close to Artemis, and even associated with her on occasion, was Hecate, mysterious goddess of magic arts. She had power over the shades of the dead, sent demons and ghosts to terrify the living, and, when invoked, could instruct human beings in the rites of magic and sorcery. She was worshipped at night, in secret rites which undoubtedly included dancing. Pan, the ancient god of nature and patron of shepherds, who was believed to dwell in the remote mountain fastnesses of southern Greece, was worshipped in nocturnal mysteries and dances in many parts of the Greek world. We hear also of mysteries celebrated in honour of Aphrodite, goddess of human love and fertility—notably by women, on the island of Cyprus, her reputed birthplace. Ecstatic and lewd dances to the *tympanum* were a feature of these rites.

But perhaps most important of the Greek divinities in whose worship mysteries had a prominent place were Demeter, goddess of grain and agriculture, and her daughter Persephone, vegetation goddess and queen of the dead. At the Anthesteria, celebrated as a sort of All Souls' festival at Athens, there were mysteries to Persephone alone, but on other occasions mystic rites were offered to the two goddesses jointly. The festival of the Thesmophoria, for example, was in essence a solemn tribute to Demeter and Persephone as fertility divinities, and as givers of the laws governing family life. Only matrons of high birth and blameless character might participate in its mysteries. Many of the rites were kept rigidly secret; we know, however, that dances and contests had a place in them. Aristophanes pokes genial fun at this festival in his comedy entitled *Thesmophoriazusae*. He even inserts into his play a choral ode (lines 947–1,000) with accompanying dances which he pretends are representations of some of the dancing at the festival. He would not dare, of course, to display in the theatre any real dances from the mysteries—even if he, a man, had ever seen them! He calls the dances *orgia* (948)—a word which implies both secrecy and mysticism. He portrays them as at first light and rapid, in circular formation; then sedate and measured, as the dancers invoke various divinities, then rapid again, in a double-line formation; and at last frankly orgiastic, with loud outcries to Dionysus.[4]

Sometimes Demeter and Persephone were honoured in mysteries which had associations with other deities as well. Near Thebes, and also on the island of Samothrace, they were connected in some way with the mysteries of the Cabeiri, who were protective and fertility divinities, perhaps of Phrygian origin, and whose rites, phallic and mystic in nature, were widespread in the Hellenistic period.

Greatest of all the Greek mysteries, however, were those celebrated at the famous cult centre of Demeter and Perse-phone at Eleusis, about thirteen miles from Athens. Some of the most prominent men of the Greek world underwent initiation here. After long preparation and fasting, and preliminary ceremonies in Athens, the persons to be initiated and others who were to take part in the ritual marched all the way to Eleusis, stopping from time to time at intermediate shrines. The mysteries proper occupied three days and nights, and were concerned primarily with the return of Persephone from the realm of the dead to spend a portion of the year with her mother, Demeter—a return which symbolized to their de-votees the immortality of the soul. Although the Eleusinian mysteries were very ancient (they seem to go back to Myce-naean times, or even earlier),[5] and continued down to the end of the fourth century of the Christian era, with large numbers of persons being initiated each year, yet the secrets of the rites were kept well by both the Greeks and the Romans. We do know, however, that the ceremonies were believed to assure to the initiate a joyous and serene life after death. We know also that nocturnal torch dances were a feature of the festival. Evidently in the initiation proper some of the 'secrets' were revealed in the form of a dance drama; Lucian[6] implies that it was a profoundly affecting experience to be initiated 'with rhythm and dancing'. Aristophanes, in his play entitled *Frogs* (440–59), introduces what purports to be a beautiful dance by night in the meadows of the world of the dead, by a chorus of *mystae*, or persons who in life had been initiated into the Eleusinian mysteries.

Of a somewhat different type were the Orphic mysteries. The Orphic sect seems to have taken form as early as the sixth century B.C., and to have continued to be active down to the Christian period. It claimed as its 'founder' the mythical Orpheus, who had successfully journeyed to the realm of the dead and returned to the upper world. The sect taught that the soul of man has in it something of the divine; that man normally goes through many reincarnations as he strives to lead an ever better life and to achieve union with divinity; but that by submitting to certain initiation rites he may attain this union far more speedily. The Orphic rites were akin to those of Dionysus on the one hand, and of Persephone on the other. Their most sensational feature was an orgiastic dance in which the worshippers tore living animals to pieces and ate the gory, raw flesh in a sort of communion with the life-giving deity.

It would be unthinkable for most of us today to borrow the divinities and religious practices of far-off peoples, and to add them to our own; but the Greeks did so freely, especially in times of crisis or calamity. Many of the divinities thus adopted came into Greece from the East—from Thrace, Syria, Phrygia, and Asia Minor in general. These exotic deities were particularly popular in the Hellenistic and Greco-Roman periods, i.e. from the latter part of the fourth century down into the Christian era.

Most of the borrowed cults had rituals that were ecstatic, clamorous, sensational. We hear of frenzied nocturnal dances, with crazed outcries, to the stirring accompaniment of shrill flutes, *tympana*, metal cymbals, castanets of wood, earthenware, or metal, horns, 'bull-roarers', and rattles. We hear of snake-handling, of trances, of prophesying, even of self-mutilation. Some of these rites were performed openly, while others were celebrated in private homes, by individuals and their friends, or at the meetings of clubs known as *thiasoi*.

Among the divinities from the East was the fertility goddess

Cybele, who with her consort Attis was worshipped in the mountain wilds of her native Phrygia in ecstatic dances led by emasculated priests called Galli. Rhea of Crete and the 'Great Mother' of Asia Minor were very similar to Cybele, and were often equated with her; they were invoked with noisy, often armed, dances by votaries known as Curetes or Corybantes. One feature of the rite of the Corybantes is said to have been a distinctive 'sportive' dance called *thronismos*, performed around an enthroned initiate; another was a mystic dance by means of which they claimed to be able to cure insanity. Bendis and Cotyto, Thracian goddesses, were honoured with 'mountain dances', processions through the streets, and night-long rituals. In the case of Cotyto we hear also of a rite of baptism. Adonis, visualized as a handsome young man who was beloved of Aphrodite, but who died an untimely death, was mourned by women, with loud wailing and with dancing on the rooftops. Salmoxis or Zalmoxis, a deity of the dead, was honoured with a special dance and song named for him. Sabazius was a nature divinity often confused with Dionysus; we read of wild dances to him in the streets (often performed by men and women of high social position) and of gifts of cakes to the dancers from bystanders.[7]

The orgiastic cults found disfavour among many Greeks—particularly among statesmen and philosophers. Plato, for example,[8] would impose heavy penalties upon any citizen who engaged in orgiastic rituals; and from time to time some of these rites were actually banned. They seemed, however, to satisfy an emotional need. Even Plato himself[9] says that the dances in these rituals, with their violent bodily movements, really free troubled persons from their inner conflicts and frenzy, and restore peace to their souls. In like manner Aristeides Quintilianus (2, 1, 4) regards *enthousiasmos* and 'Corybantic frenzy' as diseases of the soul, which the music and vigorous dance of the orgiastic rites themselves can cure—as the Corybantes indeed asserted.

Somewhat similar frenzied dances, with much tossing of the head, are seen occasionally in underdeveloped parts of the world today (e.g. in Africa and South America), among poverty-stricken, diseased, and hungry peoples. Some modern psychologists explain them as the outward expression of an overwhelming desire to free the spirit from the human body and to unite it mystically with deity, so that the worshipper may escape for a while the sorrows and hardships of everyday life.

VII

DANCES AT SHRINES AND FESTIVALS

SONG, dance, and processions were features of most of the religious festivals of the Greeks, from earliest times down into the Greco-Roman period. We have already considered many of such festival dances; we may here glance briefly at a few more.

Some of the dances at festivals and shrines were performed by priests, priestesses, or trained attendants of the deities concerned, while others were offerings of the people on special occasions—of *all* of the people, from small children to mature men and women, the high and the lowly alike (FIG. 37). It was not considered unmanly to dance; in fact, many men prided themselves upon being able in this way to show homage to the gods who had accorded to them strength, agility, and grace of body.

From earliest times, as we have seen, poetry was closely associated with music and the dance. Throughout Greek literature, many poems begin with an invitation to divinities, Muses, or Graces to come and observe or join in the songs and their accompanying dances.[1] Actually the development of lyric poetry was much affected by the dance—as is indicated, among other things, by the use of the word 'foot' for a segment or measure of a line of verse. In this connection a statement in Libanius[2] is often quoted: 'The songs are created for the sake of the dance.' However, this particular passage loses some of its aptness in a general connotation, for Libanius is here referring specifically to the songs used in the performances of the pantomimic dance in the late Greco-Roman period. What does seem to be true is that the Greek almost never sang or chanted verse without using an accompanying movement of some part of his body.

FIG. 37. FESTAL DANCE, EARLY SIXTH CENTURY.
By courtesy of the Walters Art Gallery, Baltimore.

We know a good deal about the various types of verse written by the Greeks for their religious rituals and dances,[3] and we have a great many actual examples of the verse. We know, for instance, that there were *hymns*, both epic and lyric, all to be accompanied by the lyre—and we have some of them. In early times the hymns appear to have been sung by a standing chorus, but this fact does not rule out the use of restrained orchestic gestures. The epic hymns, of regular, uncomplicated pattern, were probably soon accompanied by solemn processional dances of a simple choreographic type. Even the Muses engage in such dignified and beautiful processional hymns in Greek literature.[4] Lyric hymns are more complex in structure, and present rhythmic patterns which suggest a varied choreography.[5] Resembling the hymns, but more highly specialized, were *prosodia*, songs to the flute, sung by worshippers moving in a procession to a shrine, usually at the formal opening of a festival. Their purpose was in general to call the deity to be present, to beseech his favour, or to render thanks for some particular blessing to the community. There were also *nomoi*, carefully composed odes or poetic accounts of the adventures of a deity or a hero, sung by one singer or by a chorus, and accompanied by the lyre or the double flute. Like the hymns, they were at first performed without dancing, but probably always with gestures; later they seem to have been accompanied with stately steps as well as gestures. There is a record[6] of a famous *nomos*, ultimately of Lycian origin, presented each evening during a festival season on the island of Delos, by a chorus of boys who sang while another chorus, of girls, danced the meaning of the verses.

Particularly famous among the processional dances to divinities was the solemn *paean*, performed to the music of the lyre or the flute. The author of the *Homeric Hymn to the Pythian Apollo* (513–23) tells how a band of Cretans came to Delphi to establish the shrine there, singing and marching to the *paean*, with Apollo himself as their leader. The god plays the lyre and 'steps high and handsomely' (516). The *paean* seems indeed to be of Cretan origin. It was adopted by the Greeks, and used, chiefly in the cult of Apollo, as a ceremony of supplication in time of pestilence or other trouble; as a prayer before battles or other important undertakings; as a celebration of triumph after victory; or as a general expression of joy. It regularly carries the refrain 'Ie paian', the significance of which is unknown, although there have been many conjectures concerning it. On occasion the *paean* departs from a purely processional format, and becomes a 'real dance', still accompanied by song. It was especially important at the Hyacinthia and the Gymnopaedia, festivals of Apollo at Sparta.[7] At the latter, it was performed by three choruses—one of boys, one of mature men, and one of old men, all 'dancing naked and singing songs . . . and *paeans*'.[8] Sometimes it was performed by men in armour.[9] It was extended to deities other than Apollo, and often imitated in tragedy. Several songs to be sung to it are extant, and even musical notes have been preserved for some of these. The music, in the Dorian mode, suggests the dignity and stateliness which we should expect of the *paean*.

The *hyporchema*,[10] also native to Crete, was a combination of instrumental music, song, dance, and pantomime, to the music of lyre or flute or even both together. It could be performed by men or women, boys or girls. Writers repeatedly stress the fact that it was lively, rapid, flashing, joyous, fiery. Sometimes a musician both played his instrument and sang, as the chorus danced. At other times a musician or musicians furnished the instrumental accompaniment, while the chorus sang and used dance gestures or simple movements, and a smaller group of dancers performed spiritedly without taking part in the singing at all. Lucian[11] says that on the island of Delos the boys 'who have been judged best beforehand' dance *hyporchemata*—thereby implying a preliminary contest for the selection of the special dancers. The *hyporchema* was used principally in the worship of Zeus and Apollo, but also in the cult of Dionysus. It is said at times to have been a circle dance, executed around an altar during a sacrifice; at other times it seems to have been used in 'tetragonal' choruses. Its later development in Greece is something of a puzzle. It is variously reported to have been akin to the pyrrhic dance; to have been like the *kordax* of comedy; to have been concerned with mythological tales. Some scholars see a transfer of the *hyporchema* to the drama in the brief, joyous outbursts of song and dance found here and there in tragedy, and in other short and spirited songs and dances interspersed into comedy and the satyr play. Whether the singers and all the dancers finally came to form one group, we do not know.

The words of a famous *hyporchema* by the playwright Pratinas have come down to us.[12] The poem is a violent expression of resentment against the professional flute-players of his day who were departing from previous standards of ethics for their art,

FIG. 38. A PARTHENEION, OR DANCE OF MAIDENS.
In the Museo di Papa Giulio, Rome. From Adolf Furtwängler and Karl
Reichhold: *Griechische Vasenmalerei*, F. Bruckmann, Munich.

and causing the music to encroach upon the lyrics in choral performances. He begins spiritedly, 'What hubbub is this?' He calls the music 'insolence', and exclaims, as poet, 'Mine, mine is the god Bromius! Mine is the right to sing aloud!' The song is queen, he says, and the flute is only a servant. He proceeds to unrestrained invective, one imprecation of which, a made-up word, occupies a full line of verse: 'Flute-which-walks-all-over-melody-and-rhythm-babbling-grievously!' One can only speculate on the nature of the dance which accompanied this vehement outburst!

Partheneia were especially characteristic of Dorian Greek cities. They were graceful dances of choruses of maidens, in honour of deities or legendary heroes. Greek art abounds in representations of modest and beautiful young girls, dancing hand in hand or independently (FIGS. 38, 39), sometimes carrying light veils or scarves, often cloaked in flowing garments whose folds add to the charm of the choreographic pattern.

A considerable portion of a *partheneion* composed by Alcman

FIG. 39. DANCER OF THE SECOND CENTURY B.C.
By courtesy of the Walters Art Gallery, Baltimore.

for a chorus of Spartan girls at the festival of the Thosteria is still extant.[13] It is written in balancing strophes, or stanzas, of fourteen short lines each, in rapid tempo. After recounting a mythological story, the singers praise their two graceful and lovely leaders, mention several of the other maidens by name, speak of their own 'purple' garments and snakelike ornaments 'all of gold'. Oddly enough, throughout the song there is much comparison of the girls to birds (an owl, a swan, doves). Many scholars think that some of the members of the chorus may actually have been dressed or masked as birds. The performance took place at night, apparently in honour of the goddess Orthia—who was, incidentally, a bird-goddess.

One particularly attractive form of the maiden dance seems to have been the *hierakion* in Argos, in which girls carried flowers and danced to flute music at the festival of Hera Antheia.[14] It was believed that the Graces, the Muses, the Nymphs, the Horae or Seasons, and other supernatural beings engaged in similar dances.

Not maiden dances, but nevertheless distinctive songs and dances of women, were those of the famous 'invective' choruses in honour of two ancient fertility deities, on the island of Aegina. Herodotus records (5, 83) that the abusive songs of the choruses were directed at 'no man, but at the women of the region'. Ritual abuse is often associated with a fertility cult. Herodotus adds that the women of Epidaurus have similar choruses, and that 'they also have secret rites'.

The little island of Delos, in the middle of the Aegean Sea, was throughout antiquity a sacred spot, the birthplace of Apollo and his twin sister Artemis. It was noted for its magnificent festivals; and we are told[15] that no sacrifices there were un-accompanied by music and dancing. So important was the dance in the worship of both these deities that the Greeks often spoke of the divinities themselves as dancers.

We have already considered several of the dances for which Delos was famous—among them the ancient *geranos*, said to have been performed from prehistoric times by youths and maidens, alternating, in a line with hands joined (FIG. 13). This was a solemn nocturnal ritual, executed at festivals, in the flickering light of torches, lamps, and bonfires. There were many others. There were the dances of the 'long-robed Ionians', assembled on the island for the great Ionian festival; these dances were in general solemn and dignified, and sometimes took the form of contests.[16] There were many dances of maidens.

We hear of 'Delian maidens', 'handmaidens of Apollo', who sang and performed some odd vocal feat (apparently an imitation with the tongue of the clacking of castanets, together with a clever imitation of the speech of foreigners).[17] They seem also to have danced, but our information is not specific on that point.

We read that no mariners passed Delos, even when they were in great haste, without going ashore and engaging in dances in honour of Apollo. 'They quickly furl their sails,' says Callimachus,[18] 'and do not go aboard again until, under blows, they have whirled in a dance around the altar, and bitten the holy trunk of the olive tree, holding their hands behind their backs; these ceremonies the Deliad Nymph invented to furnish amusement and laughter to the young Apollo.' A ritual or dance in which performers are beaten is common among many primitive peoples; it is believed to ward off evil. Similarly, the biting of a part of a sacred tree is an old rite to avert potential danger; the Hallowe'en game of 'bobbing for apples' or 'apple on a string' seems to be a degenerated form of this ritual. The mariners' dances, then, were old 'magic' to insure the safety of their ships. The 'amusement' with which they were watched obviously came after their real significance had been blurred with the passing of the centuries.

In all parts of the Greek world, and in all periods of Greek culture, dances were offered to Artemis. We have already noted the tradition that in prehistoric Sparta a king's daughter, Helen, took part in maiden dances in her honour. The Greek traveller and author Pausanias (6, 22, 1) attests for the early worship of Artemis in Elis a lewd dance of remote antiquity called the *kordax*—the same type of dance as that of Old Comedy. At Brauron, near Athens, even in the fifth century little girls still performed ancient bear dances at one of her festivals. In Ephesus, in Asia Minor, one of the great centres of her worship in the Hellenistic age, there was a legend that the shrine had been founded in very early times by Amazons, who had set up an image of Artemis under an oak tree, and, to the shrill music of the *syrinx*, had performed two dances around it— one a combat dance, in armour, the other a circle dance.[19] It is highly probable that at the festival of the Ephesia in that place these dances may have been imitated and commemorated by armed women dressed as Amazons.

Ancient writers tell us of certain dances in the cult of Artemis, and of other divinities as well, which were held at night, and sometimes even lasted all night. We read of one such dance on the island of Samos, in which women dancers carried in their hands cakes made of sesame seed and honey, so that a group of escaped prisoners who had sought sanctuary in the temple might seize the cakes and thus avoid starvation.[20] This story sounds like an invention to explain old cake-carrying dances. Other authors mention cakes which were carried in processions and dances in honour of Artemis, Apollo, Hecate, Athena, and other divinities (cf. FIG. 40); and Athenaeus[21] says that cakes were given as prizes at nocturnal festivals to worshippers who danced to keep themselves from going to sleep, and thus succeeded in staying awake all night. These cakes were sometimes called *niketeria*, 'victory cakes'. We are reminded of the 'cake walk' at the turn of our own century; and the old slang expression 'You take the cake!' is paralleled in Greek literature.[22] All-night dance rituals are recorded also at the Hyacinthia, in honour of Apollo; in the Dionysiac cult; and in the Panathenaea, the great festival of Athena at Athens.[23]

The highlight of the Panathenaea was undoubtedly the magnificent procession up to the Acropolis—a procession in which all levels of the citizenry were represented, in festal garb. Second only to this seems to have been the performance of the pyrrhic or armed dance.

We have seen how the armed dance is found from very ancient times in Crete, Greece, and Asia Minor. We have observed that it begins as a leaping and noise-making ritual designed to drive off evil spirits and to encourage the crops to grow high. It soon turns into an armed or combat dance, and in early times is performed at the funerals of warriors. It then develops into a rhythmic series of movements and postures useful in war. A special type of flute music is perfected to accompany it, and on occasion a spirited song is sung to it, either by the dancers or by a separate chorus.

FIG. 40. THIS FIGURE MAY PORTRAY A DANCER
CARRYING A CAKE.

By courtesy of the Walters Art Gallery, Baltimore.

The pyrrhic dance formed part of the training of all boys in Sparta, from the age of five, and it persisted in that city until well into the Christian period.[24] In Athens also boys were trained in the pyrrhic dance as a preparation for military

service. Plato[25] describes it briefly, with its postures and movements for attacking an enemy with bow and arrow, javelin, and
blows of all kinds, and for eluding blows and missiles 'by bending aside, ducking, leaping, crouching'. In Athens, however,
more stress seems to have been laid upon form and grace than
was the custom in Sparta. On numerous Attic vases and reliefs
(FIGS. 41, 42) we see graceful youths armed with helmet, shield,
and spear, marching precisely, turning in circular formation,
or engaged in mimetic combat. At the Panathenaea there were
competitions in the pyrrhic dance, for which each group of
dancers was trained at the expense of a *choregus*, as was the case
in the dances of the theatre.

Surprisingly, in the course of time the pyrrhic dance takes on
Dionysiac characteristics, and pyrrhic dancers are pictured
carrying *thyrsi* and torches instead of spears, and portraying
stories of Dionysus in their dance. Still later, both young men
and young girls appear as pyrrhic dancers, often wearing brilli-
antly coloured garments, embroidered in gold. Apuleius, in the
Greco-Roman period, describes (*Met.* 10, 29) such a pyrrhic
dance, with complex and graceful evolutions, now in a wheeling
circle, now in an oblique line, now in a rectangle, now in a
wedge. From at least the fourth century on, professional dancing-girls, with helmets, shields, and spears, executed so-called
pyrrhic dances as solos, sometimes lightly and gracefully, sometimes as burlesques, and sometimes with lewd gestures and
motions.[26] In Rome we actually hear of elephants performing
the pyrrhic dance![27] Ultimately the verb *pyrrhichizein*, which
means properly 'dance the pyrrhic', comes to mean merely
'dance'.[28]

In the same general category as the pyrrhic were certain
dances performed at the Gymnopaedia in Sparta, and apparently elsewhere also, under the name of the *anapale*. In this
dance nude boys, moving gracefully to the music of flute or
lyre, displayed postures and movements used in wrestling and
boxing.[29]

For festivals of various divinities of fertility—notably Demeter, Artemis, Athena, Dionysus—it was customary for a
maiden of great beauty and of good family to be chosen as

FIG. 41. DANCE OF ARMED WARRIORS.
By courtesy of the Walters Art Gallery, Baltimore.

Basket-bearer, to carry on her head a basket containing sacred objects, in the festal procession. The title of Basket-bearer was as much prized by Greek girls as is the title of 'beauty queen' by girls today. In this connection statements in two authors are puzzling. Eustathius (1627, 46–50) says that 'baskets dance' in certain rituals of Demeter; and Strabo (13, 5, 626) says that at festivals of Artemis in Lydia 'the baskets dance'. We have already observed that 'the basket' is listed as a figure of the tragic dance. Many scholars have connected with these statements numerous representations in art of young girls in short tunics, dancing with basket-like head-dresses (FIGS. 43, 44), and have associated these in turn with the famous Caryatides, or dancing maidens of Caryae, in southern Greece, who performed at a festival of Artemis. There are several difficulties involved, however, and we cannot be sure that these are representations of Caryatides. The 'dancing baskets', too, remain an unsolved

FIG. 42. DANCE OF ARMED WARRIORS.
By courtesy of the Walters Art Gallery, Baltimore.

problem;[30] it is possible that the expression implies merely that basket-bearing girls at certain festivals executed a stately dance.

Another dance which seems to have been featured at the festival of a fertility deity is the 'kernos-carrier'—*kernophoros* or *kernophoron orchema*.[31] We have seen that the *kernos* was originally

FIG. 43. DANCER WEARING
A BASKET-LIKE HEAD-DRESS.

From Fritz Weege: *Der Tanz
in der Antike*, Max Niemeyer,
Tübingen.

FIG. 44. DANCERS WEARING
BASKET-LIKE HEAD-DRESSES.

In the museum at Delphi. From
Fritz Weege: *Der Tanz in der
Antike*, Max Niemeyer, Tübingen.

a Cretan vessel—a pan-like receptacle bearing around its edge
several smaller vessels, in each of which might be placed a little
grain, or milk, oil, or wine, as gifts to the goddess. It was carried
in the festival of the 'first-fruits'.

We have a great deal of evidence for a dance known as the
kallinikos—'the fair victor'.[32] It was associated primarily with
Heracles, but it could be offered to some other hero or divinity
on the occasion of an athletic or military victory, or a triumph
of any sort. It could be performed by men alone, by women
alone, or by men and women dancing side by side, *anamix*. Its

choreography could be processional, winding, or rectangular. It could be brief, or it could last all night. It has a place in both tragedy and comedy.

In the cult of Heracles as Victor and Serpent-Slayer there seems to have been a type of *kallinikos* performed by young men in women's dress. This is probably the dance depicted on the cylix, or shallow drinking vessel, shown in our frontispiece. The scene in the centre of the cylix—of Heracles struggling with the serpent-like 'Old Man of the Sea'—definitely associates the dance with Heracles. We know that the dancers surrounding the central scene are men, and not women, because at this period of vase painting it was the artistic convention to show the skin of men as black, that of women as white (cf. FIG. 57). Transvestism is not uncommon in ancient rituals and dances. There was, for instance, an obscene Spartan dance called the *brydalicha*, in which men wore masks and the dress of women. In Athens, at the festival of the Oschophoria to Dionysus and Athena, at which the memory of the hero Theseus was also honoured, two noble youths dressed as women led a singing and dancing chorus, all carrying vine branches heavy with fresh grapes.[33] In this case the transvestism was explained as commemorating the tradition that when Theseus went to Crete with the youths and maidens sent as tribute to the king of Crete, he disguised two youths as maidens, to increase his striking force. His stratagem was successful; he succeeded in killing the Minotaur, and bringing all the young captives home to Athens, victoriously. The dance of the Oschophoria thus seems to be akin to the *kallinikos*.

Frequently in Greek art, especially of the Hellenistic period, there are to be seen representations of dancing women wrapped in long, heavy cloaks, with hands covered, and sometimes even with a portion of the cloak drawn across the face. The figures are of great charm, and the folds of the cloaks give a marked feeling of rhythm and movement (FIGS. 3, 30, 31, 45, 46). There has been much discussion of these 'veiled ladies'.[34] They have been interpreted as dancing Nymphs or other supernatural beings; as dancers at a festival in honour of Demeter and Persephone, or of Adonis, or of Dionysus; even as male

FIG. 45. CLOAKED DANCER.
By courtesy of the Metropolitan Museum of Art, Rogers
Fund, 1922.

dancers in female garb at the festival of the Maimakteria. The motif of the covered hands has been seen as a religious convention borrowed from the East. It is possible, however, that these attractive figures do not represent dancers of any one type, but are rather evidence of the fact that Greek women (particularly matrons), when participating in dances, were usually modestly clad. They are reminders also that some of the festivals took place in winter.

D.A.G.—H

In Dionysiac dances, and occasionally in other connections as well, there is sometimes shown what has been called 'the dance with hands joined'.[35] This was probably a brief *schema* rather than an entire dance. In it the dancer holds his or her

FIG. 46. CLOAKED DANCER.

From Fritz Weege: *Der Tanz in der Antike*, Max Niemeyer, Tübingen.

FIG. 47. PHRYGIAN VOTARY, DANCING.

By courtesy of the Metropolitan Museum of Art, the Cesnola Collection, purchased by subscription, 1874–76.

clasped hands over the head, and often bends gracefully to the right or left as the dance progresses (FIG. 47). Dancers of this type are usually (but not always) clothed in 'Asiatic' costumes, with the peaked caps, long sleeves, and trousers of Persia or Asia Minor. The *schema* would seem to have been native to the East, but to have been brought into Greece at a fairly early date. It can be seen today in the classical dances of India.

Like most ancient peoples, the Greeks had 'zodiacal' or 'cosmic' dances, in which the dance line imitated the course of the planets through the skies.[36] We do not know at what festivals these dances were performed.

Finally, we should note the joyous and spontaneous dances which marked the informal festivals in various Greek cities following upon the restoration of peace after a long conflict. Tryphiodorus (429) expresses well the feeling of the people on these occasions: 'Dances are ours,' he says, 'and the honey-breathing Muse, and no more war!'

VIII

THE DANCE AND THE PEOPLE

WE have considered at some length dances which the Greeks
performed at places sacred to particular deities, or on occasions
of great religious importance. Most of these dances were formal,
and many were impressive and beautiful spectacles. There are,
however, records of many festival dances which seem to the
modern reader to resemble rather the sports and frolics of
secular life than tributes to divinities—yet tributes they were.
A good example is the *askoliasmos*, performed at the Rural
Dionysia, in which the dancers jumped or hopped up and down
on greased wineskins, accompanied, no doubt, by the delighted
outcries of the spectators.[1] Such activities show that the dance
was very close to the lives of the Greeks, and that they danced
readily, under all sorts of circumstances. As a matter of fact,
the Greek drew no hard and fast line between religious and
secular dancing; and many of the dances in which he engaged
informally, to commemorate events in his own life or that of his
family, or merely for enjoyment, were offered also to the gods.

The Greeks, like most peoples, danced at weddings, at har-
vest-time, at vintages. Our FIG. 48, from a vase of the sixth
century B.C., probably shows a wedding dance, since the major
scene on the vase portrays a wedding procession. There has
come down to us a detailed description of a dance of the wine-
press, depicting the cutting of the grapes, the carrying of the
baskets containing them, the treading of the grapes, the filling
of the jars, and finally the drinking of the new wine.[2] The
rhythmical treading of the grapes is itself spoken of as a dance.[3]
On a child's naming-day, the tenth after birth, there were
night-long dances of women, with prizes of cakes for those who
stayed awake, as in the nocturnal dances at festivals (cf. FIG.

40).[4] At funerals there were processions of mourners, marching solemnly to the music of the flute, singing dirges, and, in very early times at least, tearing their hair, scratching their cheeks, and beating their breasts and heads (cf. FIG. 12); later, these manifestations of grief were refined into graceful dances and gestures (cf. FIGS. 49, 50).

There were after-dinner dances, some performed by professionals, others by guests, spontaneously.[5] There was a Greek

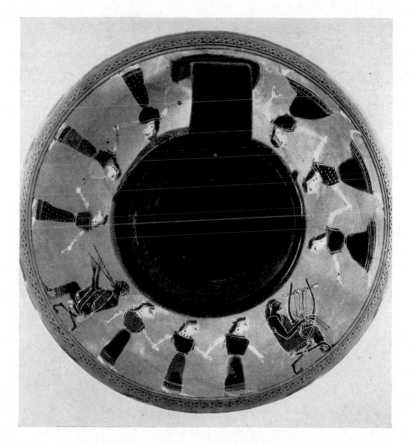

FIG. 48. WOMEN DANCERS, PROBABLY AT A WEDDING.
By courtesy of the Metropolitan Museum of Art, gift of Walter C. Baker
1956.

FIGS. 49, 50. A DANCE SHOWN IN A TOMB-PAINTING.
In Ruvo, ca. 400 B.C. From Fritz Weege: *Der Tanz in der Antike*, Max Niemeyer, Tübingen.

saying that wine makes even old men dance, against their will. Vase paintings show banqueters dancing, kicking, and whirling, slapping themselves or one another, sometimes nude, occasionally carrying wine cups or jars, often having difficulty keeping their balance (FIGS. 1, 51, 52, 53). Pollux (4, 105) apparently refers to them when he defines the *lombroteron*: 'It was a dance which they performed in the nude, with obscene language.' On occasion the banquet dances 'spilled over', as it

FIG. 51. YOUNG MAN DANCING.
By courtesy of the Walters Art Gallery, Baltimore.

FIG. 52. YOUNG MAN DANCING.
By courtesy of the Walters Art Gallery, Baltimore.

FIG. 53. AFTER-DINNER DANCE OF YOUNG MEN.
From Paul Hartwig: *Die Griechischen Meisterschalen*, W. Spemann, Stuttgart.

were, into the streets, taking the form of noisy and turbulent *komoi*, or processional dances, which kept sober citizens awake and angry.

There were, however, *komoi* of another sort—dignified and joyous processional dances, with song, in which citizens escorted to their homes victors in dramatic or athletic contests, or other local heroes. Some of the finest of Greek poets, among them Pindar, wrote odes to be sung during these *komoi*.

There were other popular dances, used on unnamed occasions. There was a dance called the *keleustes*, 'the man who sets the tempo for the oarsmen'.[6] There was a dance of the Aenianians called the *karpeia*, which portrayed the story of a farmer who is beset by a robber while driving a yoke of oxen, and who fights the intruder, sometimes putting the robber to flight, sometimes being defeated by the robber and yoked with the oxen.[7] There were dance-contests such as the Spartan *bibasis*, which consisted in kicking one's own buttocks, to music, as many times as possible,[8] and the *hekaterides* or *hekaterein*,[9] a similar dance, in which there was apparently slapping with the hands as well as kicking with the feet. There were high-kicking contests, *eklaktismata*.[10] There was a dance called the *oklasma*, said to be of Persian origin, in which the performer alternately squatted down and then stood up again, in time to music—a dance apparently not unlike the modern Russian 'squat-fling'.[11] There was a 'dance with the elbows', *epangkonismos*,[12] which recalls the 'elbow-bumping' figure which occurs in the Rüpel-tanz of Germany—and which is seen in the children's game of the 'Chicken Hop' in playgrounds of New York City to this day. There were other dances which sound like children's games—such as the *anthema*, in which the dancers, apparently in two groups, chanted: 'Where are my roses? Where are my violets? Where is my lovely parsley?' 'Here are your roses. Here are your violets. Here is your lovely parsley.'[13]

Among the Greeks, then, the dance was a social activity in the truest sense of the word. By means of it the Greek expressed all his personal and communal emotions of joy and sorrow, marked all the great events of his own life and that of his city—and thoroughly enjoyed himself. However, our common form of the 'social' or ballroom dance, done by a man and a woman together, for amusement, seems not to have appealed to him, for we have no evidence of anything quite like it in classical antiquity. Some years ago a scholar found in an antique dealer's shop in Athens two black-figured vases which he thought portrayed couple-dances in the modern manner. He published them as 'unique', and as holding a 'special place in the history of the dance'.[14] However, other students have not found his presentation convincing. Indeed, the figures on one of the vases do not actually appear to be a couple, nor to be dancing at all; rather they seem to represent one man helping another to adjust his garment.

There are two 'dances of the people' which are not now well understood, but which seem to have been of considerable importance. The first of these is one called the *dipodia*. Towards the end of Aristophanes' *Lysistrata* (1242–72), a group of Athenians and Spartans are lining up for a joyous dance. One of the Spartans addresses a musician: 'Take your pipes (*physateria*), my dear,' he says, 'so that I may dance the *dipodia*, and sing a beautiful song.' He (or the whole chorus of Spartans) then performs a dance and song in praise of the great deeds of both Athenians and Spartans in the Persian War. From the context, it seems that the *dipodia* was a Spartan dance of great beauty, suitable for a joyous occasion, but elevated in style.[15] The name *dipodia*, 'two-foot', may imply that the dance was originally performed to the Spartan trochaic dimeter, a verse line of two pairs of trochaic feet.

The other dance is the *hormos*, or 'chain'. 'The chain', says Lucian,[16] 'is a dance common to youths and maidens dancing one by one (*kath' hena*), and thus truly resembling a chain. And the youth leads, dancing agile steps and such movements as he will later use in war, and the maiden follows, dancing modestly, in womanly fashion, so that the chain is woven of sobriety and manliness.' Many writers have taken this passage to denote a dance of youths and maidens alternating side by side, with hands joined or crossed, in the *anamix* style. However, in this case, with the youths doing one kind of step and the maidens another, the result would surely be a disjointed and decidedly arhythmical jumble. It would seem that we must assume either (1) that the dancers perform with hands not joined or (2) that the dancers are aligned one behind the other, in single file, or, most probably, (3) that one youth leads a line of maidens (as in many modern Greek dances), and from time to time releases the hand of the first of the maidens and executes brilliant and spirited steps in contrast to their measured and sedate movements (cf. FIGS. 49, 50). It should be noted that in the *Lysistrata*, after the *dipodia* is finished (1273–1322), the whole company is arranged in the *anamix* formation, a man and a woman side by side all down the line, and they dance in that manner—but this is clearly a *kallinikos*, or victory dance, and not the *hormos*.

Most Greeks seem to have learned to dance at an early age, either under the tutelage of an instructor or informally, from watching and imitating their elders. The Athenian tragic poet

Sophocles, for example, was carefully trained in music and dancing from childhood, by a famous musician, and while still very young was chosen to play the lyre and lead the victory dance around the trophy after the battle of Salamis.[17] Epaminondas the Theban, one of the most distinguished among Greek statesmen and generals, was taught to play the flute and the lyre, to sing, and to dance, and he continued to perform well in these arts in his adult years.[18]

In Sparta dancing was held in very high regard, and 'was entered upon by all', both young and old.[19] In that city the *agora*, or market-place (the centre of civic life), was even called the Chorus. We have already considered many of the Spartan dances. In the training school for boys, after drill on boxing and wrestling was over, the students were formally instructed in the dance. Attention was given to the warlike pyrrhic, as a preparation for combat. The boys were also taught the stirring *embateria*—military songs and marching drills in anapaestic rhythm, to the music of the flute—which were later to be used in evolutions on the actual field of battle. The most inspired of the *embateria* were those attributed to Tyrtaeus. The words of one of them are particularly famous: 'Come, sons of citizens of Sparta, home of brave men, advance your shield with the left arm, and throw the spear bravely before you, never fearing for your life, for that is not the way of Sparta.' (Oddly enough, the ancient Greek words can be sung to the tune of 'Columbia, the Gem of the Ocean'!) Lucian[20] says that the warlike dances and marches in the schools were followed by other dances, 'such as are dear to Dionysus and Aphrodite'. To them the boys sing two songs, Lucian continues. One is an invitation to Aphrodite and the Loves to join in their dances; the other gives instructions as to how to dance: 'Step forward spiritedly, my lads, and dance ever better.' Spartan girls, also, were taught to dance; there are shocked references in Greek literature to their short, loose garments and their bare thighs as they dance in public (cf. FIG. 43), sometimes even shouting uncomplimentary remarks at young men among the spectators.[21]

The Arcadians, too, were noted for their devotion to the whole art of *mousiké*—song, dance, and instrumental music.

Training in this threefold art was compulsory for Arcadian boys from an early age, and competitions were held annually in the theatres. Girls also were trained in *mousiké*, and indeed sometimes participated in choruses along with boys—apparently in the *anamix* formation—a feature which our ancient source comments upon as something unusual.[22]

In Athens, most of the instruction in the dance seems to have been in the hands of private teachers, although boys received some orchestic training in the *palaestra*, or wrestling school. Nevertheless, several famous Athenian philosophers advocated a different approach.

Plato devoted a great deal of attention to the importance of the dance in education—particularly in his treatise on the *Laws*, where he speaks in the character of 'an Athenian stranger'. He says, in fact (2, 672 E), that the dance as a whole (including song) is identical with education as a whole, that the uneducated man is *achoreutos*, 'danceless', and that the educated man is one suitably 'endowed with the dance', *kechoreukos* (2, 654 A–B). He emphasizes, however (7, 814–17), the fact that there are two kinds of music and dance—the *noble*, imitating what is fine and honourable, and the *ignoble*, imitating what is mean or low or ugly. He would have all children, boys and girls alike, instructed from an early age in noble music and dancing, and would spur them on with contests. He would give to officials absolute power to exclude from the schools and from public performances all unworthy rhythms and harmonies, steps and gestures. Music and dancing should be consecrated to the gods, he says, inasmuch as the gods themselves dance and create dances, and their favour can be won by orchestic offerings. Noble dances should confer on the student not only health and agility and beauty of the body, but also goodness of the soul and a well-balanced mind. Plato divides the noble dance further into (*a*) dances of war and vehement action, which train for skill in tactics and for physical strength, and (*b*) dances of peace, prosperity, and modest pleasures, honouring the gods, and performed with grace, restraint, and self-control. Bacchic dances he sets apart as unfitted for Athenian citizens. Comic dances should, he feels, be performed only by slaves and foreigners. He would permit no foreigners to engage in their native songs and dances in the city unless they first meet with the approval of the officials.

Plato's great teacher, Socrates, was deeply interested in the dance, and apparently discussed it at some length with his pupils. His opinions must have inspired many of those which Plato sets forth in his *Laws*. Another pupil, Xenophon, has portrayed in his *Symposium* an imaginary banquet at which Socrates is a guest; entertainment is furnished by two professional dancers—a fact which leads Socrates to comment at some length upon their art.[23] He expresses high esteem for the dance, and recommends that it be taught more widely, for health, for complete and harmonious physical development, for beauty, for the ability to give pleasure to others, for 'reducing', for the acquisition of a good appetite, for the enjoyment of sound sleep. He confesses that he himself dances alone 'at dawn', apparently in the ancient equivalent of 'setting-up exercises', and he openly expresses the wish that he may acquire greater skill in the graceful art. Elsewhere[24] Socrates is quoted as saying that 'those who honour the gods most beautifully in dances are best in war'.

A distinguished pupil of Plato, the philosopher Aristotle, also gives some attention to the place of the dance in education. Although he would not require formal instruction in the dance before the fourteenth year, and although he would regulate it carefully so that it may serve at the same time as moral training, he would favour it as affording intellectual and aesthetic gratification of the highest type (*Politics* 8, 5–7). He points out that creative expression in general (including the art of the dance) can portray things as they are in real life, or better than they are, or worse than they are (*Poetics* 1448 A); in other words, dances can be realistic, or idealistic, or grotesque. He obviously looks with favour on the idealistic dance. Music and dance of this type can help purge the young student's soul of unseemly emotions, he says (*Politics* 8, 5–7), and can prepare the future citizen for a truly honourable enjoyment of leisure time. He makes, however, one strong reservation: No citizen should pursue these arts so far that he approaches professional status;

and, to the same end, no citizen should ever learn to play musical instruments. Here Aristotle goes beyond most Greeks, who indeed regarded the ability to play the lyre moderately well, and to sing to it, as essential for the well-educated citizen. They would agree with Aristotle, however, in relegating all professional activity in the fields of music and the dance to slaves, freedmen, and foreigners.

IX

THE DANCE AS A PROFESSION:
TRANSITION TO THE MIDDLE AGES

THE Greeks of the classical period customarily deplored professionalism of any sort, and avoided acquiring any skill to the
point where they might be associated with those who used it to
make a living. It is true that from remote antiquity we hear of
exceptionally skilful dancers; some of them—e.g. those who
were also tumblers, contortionists, and jugglers—may have been
virtually professionals. It is possible that others, especially
members of certain *thiasoi*, or groups of dancers attached to
various shrines and temples, may have approached what we
should regard today as a professional status. Members of other
groups probably resembled rather the performers in such
modern passion plays as that at Oberammergau, serving a
divinity with their highly developed talents on special occasions,
but remaining private citizens. This was certainly the case in
the *thiasos* of Sabazius, for example, in fourth-century Athens.[1]

In like manner, actors and members of the choruses in the
dramatic presentations at the City Dionysia, who even in the
best period of Greek drama were paid performers, were looked
upon not as professionals, but as special servitors or ministers of
the god Dionysus, and were accorded high respect. During the
Dionysia, indeed, their persons were regarded as sacred.

Teachers of dancing, too, who devised and taught the choreography for the ritual dances, were likewise held in the highest
regard. In early times the poets themselves, both lyric and
dramatic, often taught the dances to accompany their verses.
Sappho, admittedly the greatest of women writers among the
Greeks, is said to have taught to young girls, and to have led,
dances to her own verses.[2] The tragic poet Aeschylus was

famous for the invention of many dance figures. Thespis, Pratinas, Cratinus, and Phrynichus were not only renowned playwrights, but, even apart from their own plays, actual teachers of dancing 'to all who desired to dance'. Telesis or Telestes, who worked with Aeschylus, also invented many *schemata*. This was probably the same Telestes who could communicate clearly the whole story of Aeschylus' *Seven Against Thebes* by dancing and gesture alone, without words.[3] We have the names of other famous teachers of dancing: of Lamprus, the teacher of Sophocles, who was also one of the outstanding musicians of his day; of Calliphron, teacher of Epaminondas; of Andron, who devised a form of dancing, or interpretative rhythmical motions of the body, to be used by persons playing the flute.[4] We read of one Sannio, a dancing teacher, who, though convicted of what we would call 'draft-dodging', retained his high standing in the state by virtue of his ability to train the choruses of tragedy.[5] Shortly thereafter all those who had a hand in the preparation of plays for the great festival of Dionysus were exempted from military service.

In about the third century B.C. the poets, actors, members of the choruses, musicians, teachers, and others concerned with the production of plays became members of an association called 'The Artists of Dionysus'. This was rather a religious organization than a trade union, with a sacred enclosure and shrine of its own, at which annual ceremonies were held. Its members retained their special status as servants of the god, and were even permitted to pass without harm through hostile cities, in time of war, on their way to festivals of Dionysus.

There were, however, in classical and post-classical times, avowedly professional dancers, whose social standing was lowly but whose performances the Greeks openly enjoyed. Most of these were slaves or freedmen. Some of the slaves were themselves Greeks who had been captured in war or kidnapped and sold into slavery. Others were from Thrace, Syria, Asia Minor —often from lands as cultured as were the cities of Greece. Young slaves, especially (but not exclusively) little girls, were often purchased by 'managers' who were freedmen or foreigners. These men had the young slaves trained professionally by other slaves, freedmen, or foreigners, in dancing, acrobatics, juggling, singing, and instrumental music, and then 'hired them out' to well-to-do patrons (FIGS. 54, 55, 56). Many of the professional dancing-girls and flute-players were also courtesans.

Highly favoured as a diversion among the Greeks was the

FIG. 54. A PROFESSIONAL DANCING-GIRL AND FLUTE-
PLAYER.
From Adolf Furtwängler and Karl Reichhold: *Griechische Vasenma-
lerei*, F. Bruckmann, Munich.

dinner-party, with its ensuing *symposium*. After the meal proper was finished, the hair of the guests was anointed with sweet-smelling oil, and garlands were put on their heads and around their necks. (The *lei* is thus not exclusively Hawaiian!) They chose a 'master of drinking', apparently with much merriment, and then drank toasts to one another. A flute-player was usually present, or a lyre-player, or both. Frequently a troupe of professional dancers furnished a major part of the entertainment.

An excellent and detailed picture of the performances given by some of these professionals is set forth by Xenophon in his *Symposium*.[6] The 'manager' of the troupe, a Syracusan, brings in a flute-girl, a dancing-girl, and a boy skilled in both lyre playing and dancing. The opening 'number' is instrumental music, on both flute and lyre (2, 1–2). A little later the dancing-girl juggles twelve hoops, keeping them whirling in the air 'in rhythm', to the music of the flute (2, 8). Then a hoop is brought in, with sharp swords set upright around its perimeter. The dancing-girl turns somersaults into the hoop and out again, several times, without injury (2, 11). The boy now performs a 'beautiful' dance, and Socrates, who is a guest at the banquet, calls attention to the fact that the boy dances with his whole body, and is more handsome in the figures of the dance than when he is at rest (2, 15). A 'buffoon' who is present is suddenly inspired to burlesque the dance of the boy and that of the girl, to flute music, and gets a laugh from his fellow guests (2, 22–23). The boy sings, accompanied by his own lyre and the flute (3, 1). In passing, Socrates later points out (6, 4) that the flute-girl customarily uses body movements as she plays, to emphasize her meaning; the word which he uses, *morphazo*, is often used of dancing. Next a potter's wheel is brought in, upon which the dancing-girl is to perform a juggling or balancing trick (7, 2), but Socrates objects, and asks for a more beautiful performance, which will display the grace and charm of the young dancers. The Syracusan agrees; and soon (9, 2–7) his little troupe presents, to flute music, a mimetic dance which portrays the god Dionysus and his lovely bride Ariadne caressing each other and exchanging vows of mutual affection (9, 3, 7). So convincing and moving was their performance, says Xenophon, that the unmarried guests declared they would marry forthwith, and the married guests all got up and rushed off home to their wives! And so, abruptly the *symposium* ends.

Not infrequently courtesan dancers furnished entertainment at the *symposia*. In paintings on Greek vases we see them in scanty costume or entirely nude, dancing spiritedly to the music of the flute; often male guests watch with interest—or

FIG. 55. A PROFESSIONAL DANCING-GIRL.

A terracotta statuette in Berlin. From Fritz Weege: *Der Tanz in der Antike*, Max Niemeyer, Tübingen.

join them (FIGS. 54, 57). Sometimes male guests themselves brought courtesans to the dinner-party. Literary sources

FIG. 56. DANCING-GIRL,
POSSIBLY A
PROFESSIONAL.

By courtesy of the Metro-
politan Museum of Art,
Rogers Fund 1912.

FIG. 57. AFTER-DINNER
REVEL.

By courtesy of the Metro-
politan Museum of Art,
Rogers Fund, 1941.

occasionally refer to impromptu dances and contests staged by these visitors—including competitions in the displaying of beautiful legs or buttocks.[7] Such spontaneous performances, as we should expect, were apt to end in violent quarrels.

We have already seen that, beginning in the fourth century, courtesans often performed a version of the pyrrhic dance, with helmet, shield, and spear, or even with the Dionysiac *thyrsus*. Other dances which came to be associated with them are the so-called Ionic dances, which, in the Greco-Roman period at least, are constantly spoken of as notorious for their softness and lasciviousness.[8] In two vivid lines in a Greek poem[9] we get an arresting picture of an aged woman of this class attempting with cracked voice and unsteady movements to continue the voluptuous songs and dances of her youth.

An interesting sidelight on the dances of these ladies of dubious reputation is furnished by a bit of archaeological evidence—a vase cleverly made in the shape of a courtesan's shoe.[10] Nails on the sole seem to indicate that it was a dancing shoe—perhaps even a forerunner of the modern tap-dancer's footgear! Even more interesting is the fact that the nails are arranged so as to form the word *akolouth(e)i*, 'Follow (me)!'

It has often been pointed out that the steps and figures in which courtesans engage, as portrayed in Greek art and literature, look very much like those associated with the dances of comedy. The dancers leap and kick, they slap their own bodies, they whirl and turn dizzily. Also, there were in the *kordax* of comedy several figures (the *apokinos*, *aposeisis*, *rhiknousthai*, *kalabis*, etc.) the essential characteristic of which was a rotation of the hips and abdomen; the same movement was found in the dances of courtesans.[11] One such figure or dance is called *makter* or *maktrismos*,[12] both words being derived from *maktra*, 'a kneading-trough, tub'. We are told specifically that it involved a lascivious swaying of the hips. A similar dance, called variously *igde*, *igdis*, *igdisma*,[13] derives its name from the word for 'a mortar', which in turn goes back to a verb meaning 'grind, pound'. In this dance 'they used to rotate the hips in the manner of a pestle' (in a mortar); it also involved 'writhing, twisting'. Evidently the dance must have included both a rotation

FIG. 58. A DANCER OF THE GRECO-ROMAN
PERIOD.
By courtesy of the Walters Art Gallery, Baltimore.

of the hips, a movement which reminded the Greeks of the
stirring of a pestle, and also an occasional sharp jerk, suggestive
of pounding. It was certainly a lewd performance, and was not,
as some modern students of the dance have stated naïvely, a
'folk dance' based on the 'work rhythms' of pounding food in a
mortar. It seems oddly like the 'grinds' and 'bumps' of our own
burlesque shows!

In a passage in Athenaeus (4, 157 A) a courtesan is called
a *theatrotoryne*, a word which appears nowhere else in Greek
literature; but *theatron* means 'theatre', and *toryne* means 'ladle,

stirring implement'. Scholars have puzzled over what a 'theatre-ladle' might be, and have proposed 'stage-thumper', or something similar, as a translation. However, the reference is probably to a dance in which the contortions of the courtesan, in the theatre, call to mind a ladle 'stirring' something in a saucepan.[14]

Roos[15] recently suggested that the dances described near the the conclusion of Aristophanes' *Wasps*, and there said to be dances of tragedy, are really dances of courtesans, used by Aristophanes to demonstrate the degradation into which some of the tragic dances of his day have fallen. Roos' theory is not too compelling; it seems probable rather that the dances in the *Wasps* are part of the *kordax* of comedy. Actually the *kordax* and the dances of courtesans are in origin and in essence the same thing—stimulating or fertility dances, the exact equivalents of which are found from primitive times in the ritual of many nature deities, of whom Dionysus, presiding divinity of the drama, was one. The *kordax* itself was performed in the cult of Artemis, who was a goddess of fertility.[16]

Male professional dancers were often young, graceful, handsome, and talented, as in the *symposium* described by Xenophon. However, there appear, particularly in the Hellenistic and Greco-Roman periods, statuettes of dwarfs performing grotesque dances (FIG. 59). Some scholars, associating these with the statement in Athenaeus (12, 518 F) that the luxury-loving people of the Greco-Italian cities of Sybaris and Croton kept dwarfs in their homes, as a fad, believe that the small creatures were trained to dance for the amusement of their masters and guests.[17] Occasionally a Negro dancer is seen also (FIG. 60).

As moral standards become lower, we find increasingly frequent references in literature to *cinaedi*, professional male dancers of marked effeminacy, lewdness, and even degeneracy. These dancers performed in Italy as well as in Greece; perhaps it was their dances which inspired Cicero to say that 'nobody dances, unless he is drunk or unbalanced mentally'.[18]

From the fourth century B.C. down into the Greco-Roman period we meet in Greek literature the complaint that the dance is deteriorating. On this subject Athenaeus cites authors from

FIG. 59. DANCING DWARF, HEL-
LENISTIC PERIOD.
By courtesy of the Walters Art Gallery,
Baltimore.

the fourth century down to his own day. He quotes (14, 628 E)
the comic poet Plato as saying that if anyone danced in the
olden days, it was 'something to see'; that, compared to the
older dancers, those of his day seemed to be paralysed! The
dances of earlier times, Athenaeus continues (14, 631 E) were
more active, and at the same time had more 'orderly beauty'—
kosmos. The dancers moved modestly (14, 628 E), and gathered
up their long garments decently (1, 21 B). Their emphasis was

FIG. 60. NEGRO BOY DANCING, HELLENISTIC PERIOD.
By courtesy of the Walters Art Gallery, Baltimore.

on the feet (1, 21 F) and the gestures of the hands (14, 629 B), not on grimaces or other extraneous elements. The dances were worthy of free men, and participation in them made men better soldiers (14, 629 B). The dancers showed the effect of severe discipline, and of excellent care of the whole body (14, 628 F). So high was the standard of popular appreciation in the earlier days that a poet or teacher who trained dancers in steps and figures that did not harmonize with the songs was immediately discredited; as a result, those who designed and taught dances became perfectionists (14, 629 B). But, Athenacus implies, all of that had changed. Even earlier, Plutarch[19] had indicted the dance of his day with similar severity, charging it with bad taste and with a conscious appeal to 'stupid and foolish spectators'.

The dance was certainly changing. Here and there in the Hellenistic and Greco-Roman periods we see fleeting hints of dance themes or concepts which seem medieval rather than Greek. We may notice here but one of these—the theme of the 'Dance of Death', which later reached great popularity in the Middle Ages.[20] On two Alexandrian Greek silver cups buried by the eruption of Vesuvius in A.D. 79 and found in modern times, there are portrayed skeletons engaged in various activities of life—among them two which are dancing. The theme of the vases, clarified by inscriptions upon them, is 'Enjoy life, for the morrow is uncertain'.

We have observed how the choruses and choral dances of tragedy and comedy gradually lost their importance and their original character. In the first century of the Christian era, Apollonius of Tyana visited the theatre in Athens during the Dionysiac festival of the Anthesteria. Expecting to hear and see dignified and beautiful songs and dances from classical tragedy and comedy, he found the performers, in flamboyant costumes of yellow, purple, and scarlet, engaged in soft and effeminate dances to flute music, in which they impersonated Horae, Nymphs, and Bacchantes, and even winds and ships.[21] Apollonius rebuked the Athenians severely for their 'modern' dances—apparently to no effect whatsoever!

But even in the very period in which Greek tragedy and Greek dancing had, according to contemporary observers, reached their lowest ebb, there comes suddenly what amounts to a revival of both, in a somewhat different guise—in the performance of the *pantomimus*, or pantomimic dancer. This dance form attained a fantastic degree of popularity, and seems to have dominated the dance world of Greece and Rome until the sixth century of the Christian era.

Although mimicry of some sort had been present from prehistoric times in almost all Greek dancing, yet the particular combination of elements new and old, Greek and Asiatic, which appeared in the performance of the *pantomimus* made it a new genre.[22] It is said to have been 'invented' in 22 B.C. by two professional dancers, Pylades of Cilicia and Bathyllus of Alexandria; scholars generally agree that the date is at least approximately correct. Performances of the new dance form were first given in Rome and elsewhere in Italy, and then taken to Greek lands. The two 'inventors' may have been Greeks; their names are Greek, but dancers often assumed *noms de théâtre*. In any case, the themes of their dances were predominantly Greek.

The dance of the *pantomimus* was a highly stylized performance. It usually portrayed a story close to the themes of Greek tragedy, mythology, or legend, and made much use of *cheironomia*. The one dancer customarily played all the roles, in episodes separated by musical interludes. Sumptuous costumes were worn, of expensive materials, often silk from the Far East, sometimes bejewelled. The dancer wore a characteristic mask—with mouth closed, to indicate that he told his story without speaking. He danced to a collection of musical instruments which must have been overwhelming to an ancient audience, accustomed to a lyre or a double flute; it consisted of these instruments, and, in addition, *tympana* or hand drums, castanets, Pan pipes, cymbals, *sistra* or metal rattles, and the *scabellum*, a loud percussion instrument of wood and metal, operated by the foot. A chorus of offstage singers sang before and between the episodes of the dance; their libretto, known as a *fabula saltica*, was usually in Greek.

The performance in the theatre was introduced by a 'herald', who informed the audience briefly of the story to be enacted. The chorus then sang the initial portion of the libretto, following which, with a flourish, the *pantomimus* appeared, resplendent in flowing robes embroidered with gold and precious stones, and his great mask. With 'speaking gestures' of his supple hands, he conveyed all the nuances of a story of tragedy or legend. At the end of the episode, the dancer withdrew. During a short musical and choral interval he changed his costume and mask, to reappear as another character in the next scene of the story. The whole of the legend was unfolded in four or five scenes.

The performance closed in a final burst of music, and a tumult of applause.

Sometimes, instead of changing costumes, the dancer performed an even more difficult feat: he wore a swirling cloak, and by a slight re-arrangement or handling of it managed to portray vividly all the characters of the story. With a twist of the cloak, say our ancient sources, he could portray 'a swan's tail, the tresses of Venus, a Fury's scourge'. As a sort of encore after the dance proper, the *pantomimus* frequently gave a dazzling display of technical skill; he leaped violently, crouched, twisted and turned, performed breath-taking feats of balance, halted in poses of statuesque beauty. He is said to have displayed intoxicating grace, agility, strength, and virtuosity, the product of exceptional talent, long and exacting training, incessant practice, and rigorous diet.[23]

The dance presentations of the *pantomimi* bear a striking resemblance to an early stage of Greek tragedy—the one-actor phase, in which a single performer, with the aid of varying costumes and masks, portrayed a series of characters concerned in a story. The great difference, of course, lies in the fact that the tragic actor spoke or chanted, from early times, while the pantomimic dancer performed with dance and gestures alone. Greek tragedy, as a living genre of the theatre, had practically died out in Roman imperial times; its plots, at least, and some aspects of its dance as well, were saved for the theatre by the *pantomimi*.

The effect of the performances upon the public was almost unbelievable. A great deal of imagination and concentration on the part of the audience must have been essential, for the dances were stylized and artificial, deliberately avoiding realism; yet we are told that spectators sometimes sat in the theatres for whole days, watching the dancers almost as if hypnotized. They thought of the dancers as virtually divine, say our informants; and Seneca calls the craze for their performance a 'disease'—*morbus*.[24] Women swooned; high officials of the state hung on every move; and Roman emperors summoned the dancers for 'command performances'.

We have some information on the two 'inventors' of this new

type of dance. Both seem to have been slaves at the beginning
of their careers; for we read that Bathyllus was later a freedman
of Maecenas, and Pylades apparently a freedman of the
Emperor Augustus. Bathyllus inclined towards what was called
at the time *saltatio hilara*, which has been interpreted variously
as comedy, burlesque, or a style that was delicate and voluptuous. He did indeed favour female roles. His particular type of
pantomimic dance was never so popular as was that of Pylades.
That highly individualistic person was famous for his personal
beauty and his almost supernatural skill. He seems to have
been trained as both a tragic actor and a dancer. His artistic
standards were high. He favoured the 'grand style', akin to that
of tragedy; this type of dance came to be called *saltatio Italica*.
He was immediately and sensationally successful. He was
lionized, and, in spite of his lowly social status, was an intimate
friend of men high in political power. He went off on performing tours, he opened a school of dancing, he wrote a book
on his art, and he became immensely wealthy. Innumerable
imitators arose, and his partisans and those of his rivals often
battled in the streets of Rome. He feared no man, from the
Emperor down. He is said on one occasion to have torn off his
mask and rebuked his audience when it failed to respond as he
felt it should; he is also said to have directed an obscene gesture
at a member of another audience, who had hissed him. Augustus banished the irrepressible dancer for a short time, but soon
recalled him, apparently by popular demand.

None of the rivals or early successors of Pylades seems to
have approached him in ability—not even the famous *pantomimus* of Nero's reign. This dancer (probably one of several
called Paris), when challenged by the Cynic Demetrius, performed, without orchestra, chorus, or libretto, the whole story
of the loves of Ares and Aphrodite so clearly that the amazed
and convinced Demetrius called out, 'Man (*anthrope*)! I *hear*
what you are doing! Not only do I see you, but you seem to me
to be speaking with your very hands!'[25]

In the year A.D.2 there was set up at Naples a series of Greek
games in honour of the Emperor Augustus, and called the
Sebasta. Soon after the death of Augustus in A.D. 14 these games

were expanded to include musical and dramatic contests. Among the contests was one for pantomimic dancers, in which the prize was the princely sum of 4,000 drachmae. During most of the first Christian century these games ranked in importance with the great games of Greece.[26]

The history of the pantomimic dances is an eventful and turbulent one. Their popularity spread over the entire Greco-Roman world. The performers became notably corrupt and their performances deliberately erotic, sensational, or horrifying. Women of low repute sometimes joined the ranks of the dancers—and even, surreptitiously, women of high rank also. At least one scholar has ventured the suggestion that the actual dance which Salome performed for Herod was a pantomimic version of the dance of the Thracian Nymphs around the severed head of the mutilated Orpheus![27] The dances themselves were sometimes used for gruesome purposes; Plutarch[28] records the fact that often condemned criminals, clad in magnificent garments and wearing wreaths, were forced to dance in the thronged amphitheatre until their clothing, treated in some unknown manner, suddenly burst into flames and consumed them in an agonizing death.

Moralists, both pagan and Christian, thundered against the *pantomimi*, but still the public remained devoted to them. Some Roman emperors favoured them: Caligula, indeed, was enthralled by them, Nero aspired to be one of them, Commodus took part in their dances. Other emperors opposed them: Tiberius banished them, Claudius put one of them to death after a scandal involving the Empress Messalina, Domitian had another killed for a similar reason. The conscientious Marcus Aurelius put a 'ceiling' on their high pay and production expenses. Meanwhile the Christian Church kept up an unremitting war upon them, and gradually their influence in the Western Roman Empire began to wane. In the fourth century Libanius wrote an elaborate defence of the *pantomimi*; but many of them were forced to withdraw from the cities, where the influence of the Church was strongest, and to seek a living in the smaller towns. Their public performances in the West must have been terminated by the invasions

FIG. 61. THE EMPRESS THEODORA LEADING A RELIGIOUS
PROCESSION.

Ravenna Mosaic. From Santi Muratori: *I Mosaici Ravennati della Chiesa
di S. Vitale*, Istituto Italiano d'Arti Grafiche, Bergamo.

of the barbarians in the late fourth and early fifth centuries.

Undoubtedly large numbers of professional dancers made
their way to the East—in particular to Constantinople, capital
of the Eastern Roman Empire, where spectacles and dances
continued for a long time to be immensely popular. That here
also the pantomimic dances were under fire is evidenced by an
extant speech (*Apologia Mimorum*) of the rhetorician Choricius,
who was obviously familiar with the dances in Constantinople,
and felt called upon to defend the performers against current
attacks.

Early in the sixth century there comes to the fore in that city
a young actress-dancer named Theodora, one of the daughters
of a keeper of wild beasts in the circus. With her two sisters, she
is said to have excelled in the pantomimic art. Whether they
were actually *pantomimae* or not we do not know; certainly the
dance of the *pantomimi* had undergone many changes by that
late date, and the girls may well have been of that profession.

Procopius, who speaks at some length of Theodora,[29] stresses her intelligence, her cleverness in comic portrayals, and her utter shamelessness in what we would call 'strip teases'. She was also one of the most notorious courtesans of her day. To the shocked horror of the aristocrats of Court circles, Justinian, heir to the imperial throne, met her, fell deeply in love with her, and married her. He became emperor in A.D. 527, and immediately made her empress and co-ruler (FIG. 61).

When Theodora was converted to orthodox Christianity, it might be said that, symbolically at least, the history of the Greek dance had ended, and the Middle Ages had begun.

NOTES

I. AN INTRODUCTION TO THE GREEK DANCE

1 Herodotus 6, 129.

2 Callistratus 14, 5; Euripides, *Iphigenia among the Taurians* 1143; and possibly Sappho 112, Loeb; cf. Apuleius, *Metamorphoses* 2, 7. However, this expression is usually to be interpreted as 'having a place in a choral dance'.

3 Pseudo-Ausonius, *Nomina Musarum* 6 and 9; cf. *Anth. Pal.* 9, 505.

4 P. S. Naidu, 'Hastas', *New Indian Antiquary* I, 1938, 345–61; R. M. Hughes, *The Gesture Language of the Hindu Dance*, New York, Columbia University Press, 1941.

5 D. L. Page, *Greek Literary Papyri*, Vol. I, Harvard University Press, 1942, No. 143, p. 598, lines 18–19.

6 Cf. F. A. Wright, *The Arts in Greece*, London, Longmans Green, 1923, pp. 1, 9.

7 *On the Dance* 7. Some scholars regard this essay as the work of an imitator of Lucian, but in this book we shall speak of it as Lucian's own work. Cf. also *Anth. Pal.* 9, 270.

8 *On the Dancers* 12 and 56.

9 Plato, *Laws*, 2, 653 D–E; 672 D; 673 D; cf. *Planudean Anthology* 286.

10 Plato, *Laws* 7, 816 A.

11 *Die Tanzkunst des Euripides*, Leipzig, Teubner, 1871.

12 *Dramatische Orchestik der Hellenen*, Leipzig, Teubner, 1898.

13 See Vol. II of *Antiquae Musicae Auctores Septem*, edited by Marcus Meibomius, Amsterdam, Elzevir, 1652; also *Aristeides Quintilianus, Von der Musik*, edited by Rudolf Schäfke, Berlin, Hesse, 1937; and *Aristidis Quintiliani De Musica Libri III*, edited by Albertus Iahnius, Berlin, Calvaryi, 1882.

14 All three books cited in the previous note contain illustrations of Greek musical notation, as does also Herbert W. Smyth's *Greek Melic Poets*, London, Macmillan, 1906, pp. 529–38. The general reader will find further information on Greek music in such works as Curt Sachs's *The Rise of Music in the Ancient World*, New York, Norton, 1943; and F. A. Wright's *The Arts in Greece*, London, Longmans, Green & Co., 1923, pp. 37–73.

15 A failure to observe and interpret properly various chronological and conventional aspects of Greek art has led on occasion to fantastically impossible theories with respect to the Greek dance—particularly those of Maurice Emmanuel. See, e.g., his *Essai sur l'Orchestique Grecque*, Paris,

Hachette, 1895, and the English translation by Harriet Jean Beauley, New York and London, John Lane, 1916. Cf. Lillian B. Lawler, 'The Maenads', *Memoirs of the American Academy in Rome*, VI, 1927, 70–73.

16 Cf. the introduction to *The Dance in Classical Times*, an attractive and useful booklet by Dorothy Kent Hill, published by the Walters Art Gallery, Baltimore, Maryland.

17 Cf. Lillian B. Lawler, 'Lucida Veste', *Transactions of the American Philological Association* 69, 1938, 423–38.

18 Even the Muses and the Graces sometimes wear sandals as they dance; cf. Euripides, *Iph. Aul.* 1042; *Anth. Pal.* 6, 267.

19 Cf. Lillian B. Lawler, 'A Dancer's Trophy', *Classical Weekly* 41, Nov. 17, 1947, 50–52.

20 An example of an accidental similarity to an ancient Greek dance, as portrayed in vase paintings, can be seen in an old drawing of a native Mexican Indian dance, published in *Theatre Arts Monthly* 11, 1927, page 644. The strong resemblance is due entirely to coincidence, for there could have been no connection between the two dance forms.

21 The works of all three of these scholars may be found in Volume VIII of Jacobus Gronovius's *Thesaurus Graecarum Antiquitatum*, Venice, Typis Bartholomaei Javarini, 1732–37.

22 Cf. Isadora Duncan, *My Life*, New York, Liveright, 1933, 10–21, 55, 80, 116–53 and *passim*; *Ruth St. Denis—An Unfinished Life*, New York and London, Harper & Bros., 1939, p. 16 and *passim*; Ted Shawn, *Ruth St. Denis, Pioneer and Prophet*, San Francisco, Nash, 1920, Vol. I, pp. 20, 68–72, 73, 79–83; Vol. II, Plates xxxvii, xlii, xliii, xliv; E. Jaques-Dalcroze, The Jaques-Dalcroze Method of Eurhythmics, London, Novello, 1920, Vol. I, Preface.

23 Plutarch, *Quaest. Conv.* 9, 747 A–748 E.

24 Cf. Lillian B. Lawler, '*Phora, Schema, Deixis* in the Greek Dance', *Transactions of the American Philological Association* 85, 1954, 148–58.

25 Plutarch, *Quaest. Conv.* 8, 732 F.

26 Pollux 4, 105.

27 Athenaeus 14, 629 F–630 A.

28 Hesychius, s.vv. *krinon, botrydon*. Cf. Ernst Riess, 'Hesychiana', *Classical Weekly* 37, 1944, 240–1; Lillian B. Lawler, 'The Lily in the Dance', *American Journal of Philology* 65, 1944, 75–80.

29 Libanius, *On the Dancers* 57.

30 Pollux 4. 95–98 *passim*.

31 Cf. Julius Caesar Scaliger, *On Comedy and Tragedy* (above, note 21) 1523 C.

32 Herodotus 2, 171.

33 Hesychius, s.v. *deikeliktai*; Athenaeus 14, 621 E–F.

34 *On the Dancers* 66, 68, 70, 71, 113.

II. THE DANCE IN PREHISTORIC CRETE

1 The dates here given have recently been subjected to close scrutiny and discussion, particularly the date of the fall of the Cretan civilization, which some scholars set at 1200 B.C.; see, e.g., Emily Vermeule, 'The Fall of Knossos and the Palace Style', *American Journal of Archaeology* 67, 1963, 195–9.

2 Cf. Vincent Scully, *The Earth, The Temple, and The Gods*, New Haven and London, Yale University Press, 1962, pp. 13, 16, 108.

3 See Lillian B. Lawler, 'The Dance in Ancient Crete', *Studies Presented to David M. Robinson*, St. Louis, Mo., Washington University, 1951, Vol. I, 23–51.

4 Strabo 10, 3, 6–8, 11, 19–23.

5 Lucian, *On the Dance* 8.

6 Strabo 10, 3, 7; 19–23.

7 Strabo 10, 3, 16.

8 Eustathius 893, 37, on *Iliad* 12, 77; Schol. Pindar, *Pyth.* 2, 127; Hesychius, s.v. *prylin*.

9 Duncan Mackenzie, 'Cretan Palaces and the Aegean Civilization', *Annual of the British School at Athens* 12, 1905–6, 249.

10 Cf. F. Matz, 'Minoan Civilization: Maturity and Zenith', in *The Cambridge Ancient History*, 1962 Edition, Cambridge University Press, Vol. II, Chapter XII.

11 For example, on the Isopata ring: Sir Arthur Evans, *The Palace of Minos*, London, Macmillan, 1921–35, Vol. III, Fig. 38, p. 68.

12 Evans, *op. cit.* (note 11), III, Fig. 41, p. 72; Lillian B. Lawler, 'The Dancing Figures from Palaikastro—A New Interpretation', *American Journal of Archaeology* 44, 1940, 106–7; cf. T. B. L. Webster, *From Mycenae to Homer*, London, Methuen, 1958, p. 47 and note 2; p. 62 and note 2.

13 Lillian B. Lawler, 'The Lily in the Dance', *American Journal of Philology* 65, 1944, 75–80; Ernst Riess, 'Hesychiana', *Classical Weekly* 37, 1944, 240–1; Libanius, *On the Dancers* 116, 118; Athenaeus 3, 114 F.

14 D. G. Hogarth, 'The Zakro Sealings', *Journal of Hellenic Studies* 22, 1902, Fig. 8, No. 20, p. 79.

15 Axel W. Persson, *The Religion of Greece in Prehistoric Times*, Berkeley and Los Angeles, University of California Press, 1942, 76–79, and Plate 24, p. 179. Some scholars do not believe that these figures are masked dancers.

16 A. B. Cook, *Zeus*, Cambridge University Press, 1914–40, Vol. I, 472–95; T. B. L. Webster, *op. cit.* (note 12), 55–56.

17 See Lillian B. Lawler, 'The *Geranos* Dance—A New Interpretation', *Transactions of the American Philological Association* 77, 1946, 112–30.

18 Evans, *op. cit.* (note 11), Vol. IV, Fig. 139, p. 177; Figs. 149 and 150, pp. 194–5.

19 Matz, *op. cit.* (note 10), *passim*.

20 Athenaeus 15, 678 A–B; *Etymologicum Magnum*, s.vv. *Hellotia, Hellotis*;

Schol. Pind. *Ol.* 13, 40; Hesychius, s.vv. *Hellotia* and *hellotis*; Lillian B. Lawler, 'A Necklace for Eileithyia', *Classical Weekly* 42, 1948, 2–6.

21 S. Xanthoudides, 'Cretan Kernoi', *Annual of the British School at Athens* 12, 1905–6, 9–23.

22 Pollux 4, 103; Athenaeus 14, 629 D.

23 Evans, *op. cit.* (note 11), Vol. II, 720–5 and Plate XII.

24 Strabo 10, 3, 10–11; Diodorus 5, 77, 3; cf. Martin P. Nilsson, *The Minoan-Mycenaean Religion*, 2nd ed., Lund, Gleerup, 1950, 576–7; Axel W. Persson, *op. cit.* (note 15), pp. 148–50.

25 Evans, *op. cit.* (note 11), Vol. IV, 24–27.

26 Athenaeus 5, 180 F–181 B.

27 Fernand Chapouthier, 'Deux épées d'apparat découvertes en 1936 au palais de Mallia', *Études crétoises* 5, 1938, 1–62.

28 Cf. Angelo Mosso, *The Palaces of Crete and Their Builders*, New York, Putnam; London, Unwin, 1907, p. 322.

29 Callimachus, *Hymn. Iov.* 8; cf. the Epistle of St. Paul to Titus, I, 12.

III. THE DANCE IN MYCENAEAN AND PRE-CLASSICAL GREECE

1 Michael Ventris and John Chadwick, *Documents in Mycenaean Greek*, New York, Cambridge University Press, 1956.

2 Cf. *Iliad* 23, 130–4; Schol. Pind. *Pyth.* 2, 127; Marius Plotius, *De Metris*, p. 498 Keil.

3 Cf. Plutarch, *Theseus* 31, 2.

4 *Iliad* 16, 179–83.

5 On *Iliad* 18, 590–606.

6 *Theseus* 21.

7 On *Iliad* 18, 590–606.

8 Lillian B. Lawler, 'The *Geranos* Dance—A New Interpretation', *Transactions of the American Philological Association* 77, 1946, 112–30.

9 Even today the Koreans have a ball-playing dance.

10 Athenaeus 1, 20 F.

11 See Ernst Buschor, *Greek Vase Painting*, New York, Dutton, 1922, Plate L, Fig. 92, facing p. 100.

12 E. R. Dodds, *Euripides, Bacchae*, Oxford, Clarendon Press, 1960 ed., pp. xi–xxviii and 87; Lillian B. Lawler, 'Dance Mania in Prehistoric Greece', *Classical Outlook* 24, 1947, 38–39.

13 Apollodorus 2, 2, 2; Bacchylides X (Jebb); Diodorus 4, 68, 4; Pausanias 2, 7, 8; 2, 18, 4–7; 5, 5, 10; 8, 18, 3, 7–8; Herodotus 9, 34.

14 George E. Mylonas, *Eleusis and the Eleusinian Mysteries*, Princeton University Press, 1961, pp. 53, 224–85; Axel W. Persson, *The Religion of Greece in Prehistoric Times*, Berkeley and Los Angeles, University of California Press, 1942, pp. 148–50; T. B. L. Webster, *From Mycenae to Homer*, London, Methuen, 1958, p. 125.

15 All of the Cypriote figures mentioned here may be seen in John L.

Myres's *Handbook of the Cesnola Collection of Antiquities from Cyprus*, New York, Metropolitan Museum of Art, 1914.

16 *Jahrbuch des archaeologischen Instituts*, 1887, Taf. 3.

IV. ANIMAL DANCES

1 *Anth. Pal.* 9, 189.

2 Cf. Curt Sachs, *World History of the Dance*, New York, Norton, 1937, pp. 9–11; D'Arcy W. Thompson, *A Glossary of Greek Birds*, London, Milford, 1936, p. 264; Max von Boehn, *Der Tanz*, Berlin, Wegweis, 1925, pp. 7–8; Richard Wallaschek, *Primitive Music*, London and New York, Longmans Green, 1893, p. 242; W. O. E. Oesterley, *The Sacred Dance*, New York, Macmillan, 1932, p. 18.

3 Cf. Marjorie K. Rawlings, *The Yearling*, New York, Scribner's, 1938, pp. 94–95.

4 Cf. A. B. Cook, 'Animal Worship in the Mycenaean Age', *Journal of Hellenic Studies* 14, 1894, pp. 81–169; although published some time ago, and superseded in part by later discoveries, this is an interesting and challenging study.

5 Aelian, *Nat. Hist.* 15, 28; Pollux 4, 103; Aristotle, *Hist. Animal.* 8, 12; Athenaeus 9, 390 F, 391 A and D; 14. 629 F.

6 Aristophanes, *Wasps* 1479, 1490.

7 Athenaeus 8, 360 B–D.

8 Porphyrius, *De Abstinent.* 4, 16; Pseudo-Augustinus, *Quaest. Vet. et Nov. Test.* 114, 'Adversus Paganos'; cf. also Cook, *op. cit.* (note 4), pp. 117–19.

9 Euripides, *Bacchae* 698, 767–8 and *passim*.

10 Demosthenes, *On the Crown* 260; cf. also Plutarch, *Alexander* 2.

11 Cyprian, *Confessio* 1; cf. Eudocia, *De S. Cypriano* 2, 20–21; A. B. Cook, *Zeus*, Cambridge University Press, 1914–40, Vol. III, p. 775 and notes 4 and 5.

12 J. P. Vogel, *Indian Serpent-Lore*, London, Probsthain, 1926, p. 274; Lewis R. Farnell, *Cults of the Greek States*, Oxford University Press, 1896, Vol. III, 327–8; 89.

13 Strabo 9, 3, 10; Plutarch, *Moralia* 293 C; 417 F and schol.; 418 A–B; Aelian, *Var. Hist.* 2, 1; Pollux 4, 84.

14 Aristophanes, *Wasps* 1169; cf. Anacreon, Frag. 57, Edmonds.

15 Velleius Paterculus 2, 83.

16 *Annual of the British School at Athens* 13, 1906–7, pp. 392–5 and Plate 14; Guy Dickins, *Hellenistic Sculpture*, Oxford, Clarendon Press, 1920, p. 62 and Fig. 48.

17 Aristophanes, *Lysistrata* 645 and schol.; Suidas, s.v. *arktos*; Euripides, Frag. 767 Nauck; Pausanias 3, 18, 4; Bekker, *Anecd.* I, 444–5, s.v. *arkteusai*.

18 John Papadimitriou, 'Iphigeneia at Brauron', *Classical Journal* 58, 1962, 70–71, reprinted from *The London Times* for September 28, 1961.

19 *Annual of the British School in Athens* 12, 1905–6, p. 323 and Fig. 3 K; A. B. Cook, *Zeus*, Cambridge University Press, 1914–40, Vol. III, p. 1068.

20 Porphyrius and Pseudo-Augustinus, *locis citatis* (note 8).

21 Proll. to Theocritus, Ahrens, Vol. II, p. 5.

22 Herodotus 5, 6; *Anth. Pal.* 7, 10, 3.

23 Athenaeus 5, 198 E.

24 Achille Vogliano, 'La grande iscrizione Bacchica del Metropolitan Museum', *American Journal of Archaeology* 27, 1933, 215–31.

25 Hesychius, s.v. *nibatismos*; cf. s.v. *nibades*; Athenaeus 14, 629 D.

26 Johannes Meursius, 'Orchestra', in Jacobus Gronovius's *Thesaurus Graecarum Antiquitatum*, Venice, 1732–7, Vol. VIII, s.v. *nibatismos*.

27 Cook, 'Animal Worship' (see note 4), pp. 149–50.

28 Athenaeus 12, 520 C–F.

29 Cook, *Zeus* (see note 19), Vol. I, Plate xxx, facing p. 497.

30 Lillian B. Lawler, 'Orchesis Phobera', *American Journal of Philology* 67, 1946, pp. 67–70.

31 *Pyth.* 10, 36; *Frag.*, p. 560 Sandys.

32 Cf. Lillian B. Lawler, 'Proteus Is a Dancer', *Classical Weekly* 36, 1943, pp. 116–17; Libanius, *On the Dancers* 56 and 117.

33 Cf. E. K. Chambers, *The Mediaeval Stage*, Oxford University Press, 1093, Vol. I, Chapter I and frontispiece.

V. THE DANCE AND THE DRAMA

1 Gerald F. Else, *Aristotle's Poetics: The Argument*, Harvard University Press, 1957; Gerald F. Else, 'The Origin of *Tragoedia*', *Hermes* 85, 1957, 17–46; Martin P. Nilsson, 'Der Ursprung der Tragödie', in *Opuscula Selecta*, Lund, Gleerup, 1951, 61–145; Margarete Bieber, *The History of the Greek and Roman Theater*, 2nd ed., Princeton University Press, 1961; Peter D. Arnott, *An Introduction to the Greek Theatre*, London, Macmillan, and New York, St. Martin's Press, 1959; Roy C. Flickinger, *The Greek Theater and Its Drama*, 4th ed., University of Chicago Press, 1936; Francis M. Cornford, *The Origin of Attic Comedy*, London, Edward Arnold, 1914; Sir William Ridgeway, *The Origin of Tragedy*, Cambridge University Press, 1910; Jane E. Harrison, *Themis*, Cambridge University Press, 1912; A. W. Pickard-Cambridge, *Dithyramb, Tragedy, and Comedy*, Oxford, Clarendon Press, 1927; 2nd edition, 1962.

2 T. B. L. Webster, *From Mycenae to Homer*, London, Methuen, 1958, 49–51 and 293.

3 Epicharmus, ap. Athenaeus 14, 628 B.

4 Archilochus, Frag. 77 Diehl.

5 *Poetics* 1449 A, 9–15.

6 Webster, *op. cit.* (note 2), p. 53.

7 Cf. *Anth. Pal.* 7, 410.

8 Hesychius, s.v. *tyrbasia*; Pollux 4, 105.

9 Schol. on Plato, *Republic* 3, 394 C.

10 For the masks, costumes, and footwear of tragic actors and members of the chorus, see A. W. Pickard-Cambridge, *The Dramatic Festivals of Athens*, Oxford, Clarendon Press, 1953, pp. 175–238.

11 Athenaeus 1, 21 F and 22 A; cf. a similar feat in much later times, as recorded by Lucian, *On the Dance* 63.

12 Athenaeus 1, 20 F, 21 E–F, 22 A; Plutarch, *Quaest. Conv.* 8, 9, 3, 732 F.

13 Schol. *Hecuba* 647, p. 211 Dindorf.

14 Lillian B. Lawler, 'Cosmic Dance and Dithyramb', *Studies in Honor of Ullman*, St. Louis University, 1960, 12–16.

15 Aristotle, *Poetics* 1456 A, 29–30.

16 Philodemus, *De Mus.* 4, 7, 1–8, p. 70 Kemke.

17 Plato, *Laws* 2, 670 D; 7, 798 D–816 E; Athenaeus 14, 628 D–629 B; Pseudo-Plutarch, *De Musica* 1131–47, *passim*.

18 Pollux 4, 99; Athenaeus 1, 20 E; Hesychius, s.v. *kordax*; Lucian, *On the Dance* 26.

19 Aristophanes, *Thesmophoriazusae* 947–1000; *Frogs* 316–459.

20 Athenaeus 7, 276 A; 10, 448 B; 10, 453 C–F and 454 A; Lillian B. Lawler, 'The Dance of the Alphabet', *Classical Outlook* 18, 1941, 69–71.

21 *Papyrus Bodmer IV, Ménandre: Le Dyscolos*, Publié par Victor Martin, Geneva, Bibliotheca Bodmeriana, 1958. An English translation by Gilbert Highet, under the title 'The Curmudgeon', may be found in the magazine *Horizon*, I, No. 6, July, 1959, 78–88; another, by W. G. Arnott, under the title *Menander's Dyskolos, or The Man Who Didn't Like People*, is published by the University of London, Athlone Press, 1960.

22 For an understanding of the origin and nature of the satyr play see Flickinger, *op. cit.* (note 1), 23–33 and *passim*; Pickard-Cambridge, *Dramatic Festivals* (note 10), *passim*; Bieber, *op. cit.* (note 1), *passim*.

VI. OTHER ORGIASTIC AND MYSTERY DANCES

1 Schol. on Euripides' *Hecuba* 934. This probably is the ecstatic dance referred to by Vergil in *Georg.* 2, 487–8: '. . . virginibus bacchata Lacaenis Taygeta . . .'

2 Cf. Martin P. Nilsson, *Griechische Feste von religiöser Bedeutung*, Leipzig, Teubner, 1906, 246–7.

3 Cf. Kurt Latte, 'De Saltationibus Graecorum Capita Quinque', *Religionsgeschichtliche Versuche und Vorarbeiten* 13 (1913), 102.

4 Lillian B. Lawler, 'Diple, Dipodia, Dipodismos in the Greek Dance', *Transactions of the American Philological Association* 76, 1945, 59–73.

5 George E. Mylonas, *Eleusis and the Eleusinian Mysteries*, Princeton University Press, 1961, 14–20; Axel W. Persson, *The Religion of Greece in Prehistoric Times*, Berkeley and Los Angeles, University of California Press, 1942, 148–50; T. B. L. Webster, *From Mycenae to Homer*, London, Methuen, 1958, 125. There was a tradition that all mysteries were ultimately of Cretan origin; cf. Diodorus 5, 77, 3.

6 *On the Dance* 15.

7 Demosthenes, *On the Crown* 259–60.

8 Plato, *Laws* 10, 910 B–C; cf. also 7, 815 C.

9 Plato *Laws* 7, 790–1 A–B.

VII. DANCES AT SHRINES AND FESTIVALS

1 Sappho, Frags. 60 and 65 Bergk; Anacreon, Frag. 69 Bergk; Pindar, *Ol.* 14, 1–20.

2 *On the Dancers* 88.

3 Cf. Herbert W. Smyth, *Greek Melic Poets*, London, Macmillan, 1906, pp. xvii-cxxxiv.

4 Hesiod, *Theogony* 63–71.

5 For ancient musical settings of two hymns to Apollo see Smyth, *op. cit.* (note 3), pp. 529–38.

6 Callimachus, *Hymn IV, To Delos*, 300–6.

7 Xenophon, *Hellenica* 4, 5, 11; *Agesilaus* 2, 17.

8 Athenaeus 15, 678 C; 14, 630 D–E.

9 Xenophon, *Anabasis* 6, 1, 11.

10 Plutarch, *Quaest. Conv.* 9, 748 A–B; Athenaeus 1, 15, D–F; 5, 181 B; 14, 617 B–F; 14, 630 D–E; 14, 631 C–D; Lucian, *On the Dance* 16; Heliodorus 3, 2–3.

11 Lucian, *On the Dance* 16.

12 Athenaeus 14, 617 B–F.

13 Frag. 23 Bergk; H. W. Smyth, *op. cit.* (note 3), pp. 175–82; cf. Lillian B. Lawler, 'The Dance of the Holy Birds', *Classical Journal* 37, 1942, pp. 351–61.

14 Pollux 4, 78.

15 Lucian, *On the Dance* 16.

16 Lillian B. Lawler, 'Orchesis Ionike', *Transactions of the American Philological Association* 74, 1943, 60–71.

17 *Homeric Hymn to the Delian Apollo* 146–64.

18 Callimachus, *Hymn IV, To Delos* 316–24 and schol.; Hesychius, s.v. **Delkakos bomos*; Lillian B. Lawler, 'The Dance of the Ancient Mariners', *Transactions of the American Philological Association* 75, 1944, 20–23.

19 Callimachus, *Hymn III, To Artemis*, 237–47.

20 Herodotus 3, 48, 2.

21 14, 647 C; 15, 668 C–D.

22 Aristophanes, *Knights* 277; *Thesmophoriazusae* 94; cf. also Lawler, 'Orchesis Ionike' (note 16).

23 Euripides, *Bacchae* 485–6; *Heraclidae* 777–83.

24 Athenaeus 14, 630 D, 631 A–B; cf. Lucian, *On the Dance* 10.

25 *Laws* 7, 815 A.

26 Xenophon, *Anabasis* 6, 1, 12–13; cf. Athenaeus 14, 629 F, where the pyrrhic is included among humorous dances.

27 Pliny, *Nat. Hist.* 8, 2, 5.

28 Plutarch, *De Ser. Num. Vind.* 554 B.

29 Athenaeus 14, 631 B.

30 The whole subject is treated extensively by A. B. Cook, in *Zeus*, Cambridge University Press, 1914–40, Vol. III, 975–1015.

31 Pollux, 4, 103; Athenaeus 14, 629 D.

32 Lillian B. Lawler, 'Orchesis Kallinikos', *Transactions of the American Philological Association* 79, 1948, 254–67.

33 Plutarch, *Theseus* 22–23; Athenaeus 14, 631 B.

34 Heinrich Heydemann, 'Über eine verhüllte Tänzerin', *Hallisches Winckelmannsprogramm* IV, 1879; Louis Séchan, *La danse grecque antique*, Paris, De Boccard, 1930, 129–34.

35 Maurice Emmanuel, *Essai sur l'Orchestique Grecque*, Paris, Hachette, 1895, 210–18; Séchan, *op. cit.* (note 34), 172–5.

36 Schol. Euripides, *Hecuba* 647, p. 211 Dindorf; Schol. Aristophanes, *Clouds* 563; *Et. Mag.* 690, 47; Lillian B. Lawler, 'Cosmic Dance and Dithyramb', *Studies in Honor of Ullman*, St. Louis University, 1960, 12–16.

VIII. THE DANCE AND THE PEOPLE

1 Pollux 9, 21.

2 Longus, *Daphnis and Chloe* 2, 36, and 4, 38.

3 *Anth. Pal.* 11, 64 and 9, 403.

4 Athenaeus 14, 668 D; cf. Kurt Latte, 'De Saltationibus Graecorum Capita Quinque', *Religionsgeschichtliche Versuche und Vorarbeiten* 13, 1913, 73–75.

5 Xenophon, *Symposium* 2, 21–22; Athenaeus 4, 134 A–C.

6 Athenaeus 14, 629 F.

7 Xenophon, *Anabasis* 6, 1, 7–8.

8 Pollux 4, 102.

9 Athenaeus 14, 630 A; Pollux 4, 102; Hesychius, s.v. *hekaterein*.

10 Pollux 4, 102.

11 Lillian B. Lawler, 'Four Dancers in the *Birds* of Aristophanes', *Transactions of the American Philological Association* 73, 1942, 60–61.

12 Athenaeus 14, 630 A; cf. Lillian B. Lawler, 'Dancing with the Elbows', *Classical Journal* 38, 1942, 161–3.

13 Athenaeus 14, 629 E.

14 A. Philadelpheus, 'Une Représentation du "Pas de Deux" sur Deux Vases Antiques', *Bulletin de Correspondance Hellénique* 64–65, 1940–1, pp. 34–35.

15 Lillian B. Lawler, 'Diple, Dipodia, Dipodismos in the Greek Dance', *Transactions of the American Philological Association* 76, 1945, 66–73.

16 *On the Dance* 12.

17 Athenaeus 1, 20 F.

18 Nepos, *Epaminondas*, Praefatio and Sec. 2.

19 Libanius, *On the Dancers* 17.

20 *On the Dance* 11.

21 Plutarch, *Lycurgus* 14, 2–3; Euripides, *Andromache* 595–601.

22 Athenaeus 14, 626 B–E.

23 Xenophon, *Symposium* 2, 12–20. See also our following chapter.

24 Athenaeus 14, 628 F; cf. 1, 20 F.

IX. DANCE AS A PROFESSION: TRANSITION TO MIDDLE AGES

1 Demosthenes, *On the Crown* 259–60.

2 Sappho, Frag. 40 Edmonds; cf. *Anth. Pal.* 9, 189.

3 Athenaeus 1, 21, D–F; 22 A.

4 Athenaeus 1, 20 F and 22 C; Nepos, *Epaminondas* 2.

5 Demosthenes, *Against Meidias*, 58–59.

6 See also Athenaeus 4, 129 A–130 B, and *passim*; cf. Margarete Bieber, 'Mima Saltatricula', *American Journal of Archaeology* 43, 1939, 640–4.

7 Lucian, *Dialogues of Courtesans* 3; Alciphron, *Letters of Courtesans* 13.

8 Horace, *Carm.* 3, 6, 21–24.

9 *Anth. Pal.* 9, 139, 1–2.

10 C. F. Daremberg and E. Saglio, *Dictionnaire des Antiquités Grecques et Romaines*, Paris, Baillière, 1877–1919, s.v. *solea* in Vol. 4, Part 2; also, Fig. 4968, in Vol. 3, Part 2, s.v. *meretrices*.

11 Apuleius, *Metamorphoses* 2, 117.

12 Pollux 4, 101; Hesychius, s.v. *makter*.

13 Pollux 10, 103; 4, 101; Athenaeus 14, 629 F; *Etymologicum Magnum*, p. 464, 49–52; Suidas, s.v. *igde*; Lillian B. Lawler, 'A Mortar Dance', *Classical Journal* 43, 1947, 34.

14 Cf. Lillian B. Lawler, 'Ladles, Tubs, and the Greek Dance', *American Journal of Philology* 71, 1950, 70–72.

15 Ervin Roos, *Die Tragische Orchestik im Zerrbild der Altattischen Komödie*, Lund, Gleerup, 1951.

16 Pausanias 6, 22, 1.

17 Cf. Louis Séchan, *La danse grecque antique*, Paris, de Boccard, 1930, 227.

18 Cicero, *Pro Murena* 6, 13.

19 *Quaest. Conv.* 9, 748 C–D.

20 Cf. Carl Selmer and Vincent Aita, 'A Catalan Death Dance of the Fourteenth Century', *Classical Bulletin* 20, December 1943, 22–23.

21 Philostratus, *Vita Apollonii* 4, 21.

22 For the *pantomimi* and their dances see Vincenzo Rotolo, *Il Pantomimo*, *Studi e Testi*, Palermo, Presso L'Accademia, 1957; Lillian B. Lawler, 'Portrait of a Dancer', *Classical Journal* 41, 1946, 241–7; Ludwig Friedländer, *Roman Life and Manners under the Early Empire*, London, Routledge, and New York, Dutton, no date, Vol. II, 100–17; Lucian, *On the Dance*, is the best single ancient source on the subject.

23 Lucian, *On the Dance* 35–36, 63–65, 69, 71, 74, 77–78; Libanius, *On the Dancers* 68–69, 103–10, 118; cf. Lillian B. Lawler, 'Proteus Is a Dancer', *Classical Weekly* 36, 1943, 116–17.

24 Seneca, *Controversiae* 3, praefatio 10; cf. Lucian, *On the Dance* 78, 79, 85.

25 Lucian, *On the Dance* 63.

26 Russel M. Geer, 'The Greek Games at Naples', *Transactions of the American Philological Association* 66, 1938, 208–21; Lucian, *On the Dance* 32.

27 F. A. Wright, *The Arts in Greece*, London, Longmans Green, 1923, p. 32.

28 Plutarch, *De Ser. Num. Vind.* 554 B.

29 *Anecdota* 9, 13–14; 20; 23, and *passim*.